THE TIGER FROM POZNAŃ

To my brothers in arms

THE TIGER FROM POZNAŃ

RICHARD SIEGERT

TRANSLATED BY MACIEJ SZCZĘSNY

Pen & Sword

MILITARY

AN IMPRINT OF PEN & SWORD BOOKS LTD.
YORKSHIRE – PHILADELPHIA

This edition is taken from the Polish edition originally published by Wydawnicto Pomost in 2010 as *Tygrys Z Poznania*

First published in Great Britain in 2021 by
PEN AND SWORD MILITARY
An imprint of
Pen & Sword Books Ltd
Yorkshire – Philadelphia

ISBN 978 1 52677 917 5

A CIP catalogue record for this book is available from the British Library.

Typeset in Times New Roman 12/16 by
SJmagic DESIGN SERVICES, India.
Printed and bound in UK by CPI Group (UK) Ltd, Croydon, CR0 4YY

Pen & Sword Books Ltd. incorporates the Imprints of Pen & Sword Archaeology, Atlas, Aviation, Battleground, Discovery, Family History, History, Maritime, Military, Naval, Politics, Railways, Select, Transport, True Crime, Fiction, Frontline Books, Leo Cooper, Praetorian Press, Seaforth Publishing, Wharncliffe and White Owl.

For a complete list of Pen & Sword titles please contact

PEN & SWORD BOOKS LIMITED
47 Church Street, Barnsley, South Yorkshire, S70 2AS, England
E-mail: enquiries@pen-and-sword.co.uk
Website: www.pen-and-sword.co.uk

or

PEN AND SWORD BOOKS
1950 Lawrence Rd, Havertown, PA 19083, USA
E-mail: uspen-and-sword@casematepublishers.com
Website: www.penandswordbooks.com

Contents

Part II – Captivity

Note from the Editor to the Polish Edition

The Tiger from Poznań by Richard Siegert is another instalment in the 'Festung Poznań 1945' series. For several reasons, for me, this is the most important one: I have a special, personal relationship with this title after meeting the author by chance in 2001 and with whom I conducted a very heartfelt and sincere correspondence. I would like to thank Dr Dieter Friese, head of *Hilfsgemeinschaft ehem. Posenkämpfer,* who forwarded my letter to Richard Siegert and informed him about my interest in German armoured vehicles from the Battle of Festung Poznań. I soon received a comprehensive reply from Richard Siegert, a name I didn't know at the time, along with a signed copy of his book. On the cover was the title *Der Tiger von Posen* [The Tiger from Poznań] and the author turned out to be the ex-gunner of the only fighting Tiger tank in Poznań in January and February 1945. I still treasure my copy of the book to this day.

That's when our relationship, which I can now without any hesitation call a friendship, started, despite never meeting in person. Over the course of four years we exchanged dozens of letters, allowing us to investigate the story of Tiger and its crew, together. Richard Siegert contributed his memories, while I, living close to Poznań, helped him with numerous clues from the local area. This cooperation resulted in a book entitled *Armoured Striking Reserve – Poznan 1945,*[1] first published by Pomost Publishing in 2003.

1. Polish edition: *Pancerna rezerwa Uderzeniowa – Poznań 1945.*

The friendship which began then and developed until Siegert's death in February 2012, was a completely new and unexpected experience for me. Richard Siegert was the first German Wehrmacht soldier I'd met, bearing in mind that the Wehrmacht army had caused the Poles such great suffering and harrowing experiences during the war. Likewise, I know for him it was surprising that a 30-year-old Pole had such a strong interest in his personal story.

I wanted to find out as much as possible about the man who sent the letters and his current views on these past events. My head was filled with questions and doubts, but these were soon dispelled thanks to the other members of *Hilfsgemein- schaft ehem. Posenkämpfer*. Never have I met individuals so strongly and sincerely engaged in unifying the Polish, German and Russian people. In one of his letters from April 2005, Richard Siegert wrote to me: '2005 was declared the year of Polish-German friendship. We've been cultivating such a relationship since 2001. We're faster than our politicians!'

This is why it's been my desire to share *The Tiger from Poznań* with new readers as soon as possible. Previously only published in Germany and Poland, the story of the Tiger's crew is unbelievable and provides new and detailed information regarding the battle for Poznań in 1945.

The Polish edition was extended with additional chapters: 'Guarded by a Polish Sentry' in Part One and 'Captivity' in Part Two. There's also a new chapter regarding *Gefreiter* Alfred Leupold.

I asked the author to elaborate further on his period of captivity as I believed it would interest new readers. At the time, few memoirs of German soldiers held captive by Poles or Russians were available in Polish bookstores. However, these are only individual experiences, stored deep within the author's memory and which, as he himself claims, are unable to fully reflect the mental and physical suffering experienced by a person living on the brink of starvation and exhaustion for four years. Richard Siegert vividly describes his experiences from this period of his life and, most importantly, doesn't describe himself as an innocent victim. He was fully aware that his suffering was an inevitable consequence of Germany losing the Second World War, as well as a result of his own decisions.

Maciej Karalus
Pomost Publishers

Preface to the Polish Edition

It took nearly fifty years after the end of the Second World War for the former enemies to start developing friendly relations.

German soldiers had fought for almost five weeks in desperate circumstances in Festung Poznań, right until the bitter end. Polish people have often asked 'what for?' This very question was also posed by young Maciej Karalus, who studies these circumstances from a historical perspective. He also analysed German documentation regarding the battles for Poznań in order to search for the answer. He discovered that the main drive for the German soldiers wasn't the wish to preserve Nazism, but rather their loyalty to the soldier's oath. This is the main theme of my memoires.

I would like to thank Maciej Karalus for the work put into preparing the Polish edition of *The Tiger from Poznań* and Pomost publishing house for its publication, which was made possible thanks to the political and systematic changes that have taken place in Poland over the last sixteen years.

Richard Siegert
August 2005

Part I

Fortress Poznań

Oberschütze Richard Siegert during training with 3rd Company, 108th Panzer Grenadier Battalion. Dresden, April 1941. (*Richard Siegert*)

Introduction

Following the German army's offensive in 1941, I found myself in the middle of the front. In summer 1944 I was serving in the 664th Heavy *Panzerjäger Battalion* (*Schweren Heeres Panzerjäger Abteilung 664*), which participated in the defence of Vitebsk, in Belarus. On 23 June 1944, the anniversary of Germany's invasion of Russia, the Soviets began an offensive there, comprising of 140 infantry divisions and 43 tank brigades. The already decimated German troops didn't have sufficient resources to stop the enemy. Within two days, two German divisions in Vitebsk were obliterated.

On the eve of 1943, Richard Siegert was wounded after his Hornisse was hit by a T-34 bullet. This photograph was taken at the aid station in Vitebsk. From there he was referred to the University Clinic in Vilnius. (*Richard Siegert*)

As a result of the great battle, in which the Russians destroyed those German units trapped in the cauldron, 200,000 men were taken prisoner, including as many as 58 generals, 20 of whom committed suicide. I managed to escape two other cauldrons – Minsk and Orsha – and reached East Prussia. Out of 600 soldiers, only 10 of us survived. We managed to reach the town of Chernyahovsk, where our unit was reformed and assigned to the 1st Infantry Division tasked with defending East Prussia. I was wounded during a fight with two T-34s on the Virgin Mary Bridge in Sovetsk. Boarding the transport ship *General von Steuben*, I travelled from Królewiec to Świnoujście and saved myself from that hell. I finally arrived at a hospital in Mühlhausen, which is where my Poznań story begins.

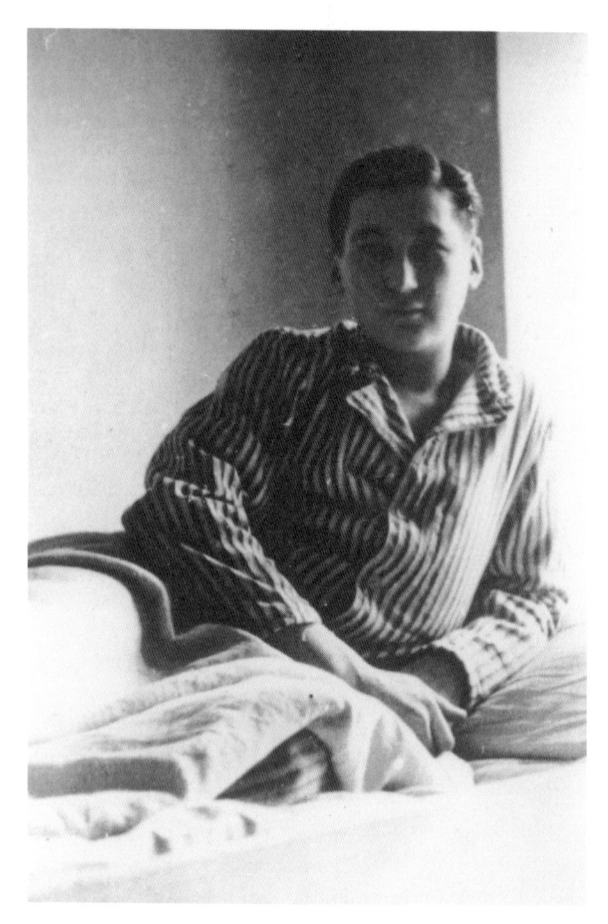

Obergefreiter Richard Siegert as a patient at the University Clinic in Vilnius. At the time, he was serving in the 664th Heavy *Panzerjäger* Battalion. January/February 1944. (*Richard Siegert*)

Chapter 1

A Hero's Return and Assessing the Situation

Obergefreiter Richard Siegert in January 1945 during his convalescence in Thuringia. That same month, he left for Poznań. (*Richard Siegert*)

On 10 January 1945 I boarded a train in Berlin heading to East Prussia. I'd returned from the hospital in Mühlhausen with an order to report to the backup unit in Olsztyn. I'd been in the military hospital, which was located in a former hostel in the forest, since October. Conditions there were awful: the rooms had no heating and there was no warm water. Due to the Allies constantly bombing the Leuna factory in Halle-Merseburg, we were more familiar with the anti-aircraft cellars than the upper floors of the building. The food was terrible: I'd lost 7.5 kg in eight weeks, despite receiving packages from home.

No wonder we'd all had enough. It was, as a *Landser*[2] would say, 'complete garbage'. Neither news from the papers nor the OKW[3] announcements were of interest, which between us we'd all decided

2. A term for regular soldiers.

3. *Oberkomando der Wermacht* – Wermacht Central Command.

were a pack of lies anyway. This lack of interest would prove to be disastrous for me as it was this ignorance about the current situation on the front that accompanied me to East Prussia. I was surprised to see men in SA uniforms, equipped with outdated rifles, board my train. They were the ones who told me about our newest weapon, the *Volkssturm*[4], which is why I was surprised when I heard the following announcement in Poznań: 'Attention! Attention! This train isn't going any further! Passengers heading to Olsztyn are asked to report to the station office for further instructions!'

So, along with other soldiers I headed to station headquarters, taking my box of belongings with me. It seemed as if we were already expected. A *Feldwebel*[5] asked us to form a line and ordered shortly: 'Unit, to the left! March!' and hurried us on. We didn't think much of it at the time and instead waited to see what would happen. In the sapper barracks at Wilda they formed us into a group of 150 and directed us to collect our rifles and take up our designated positions.

Great! At first, I thought 'not me!' I resented such sudden, unexpected commands and wasn't going to get myself killed because of some nonsensical order. During my four and a half years at the front I'd often met with similar situations. So I turned around and marched with other soldiers towards one of the barrack buildings, where I intended to disappear from sight. From the second floor, I calmly watched what was happening in the square: the allocation of weapons, equipment etc. If up to this point I was still unaware of how close the Russians were, I realised it at that moment. I felt depressed: the situation seemed hopeless. I kept wondering what I should do next. I could run, now or even later, and head back to

4. Territorial units consisting of men from 16 to 60 years old, assembled in Germany from September in order to strengthen the *Wermacht* in times of total mobilization.

5. Non-commissioned officer.

my homeland, but the hopelessness of the situation made me decide to stay. After all, it made no difference whether I fought there or in Berlin, as long as I wasn't carrying a Russian rifle in the 'vacation battalion'.

I hid my box of food in a locker in one of the empty rooms. Here, I had a good insight as to what was happening in the barracks during the day, and, in case of an emergency, I could hide somewhere. I had to give up my food rations for fear of getting caught. My supply of cake would have to suffice. I still didn't know what to do, so I just waited. Not wanting to risk anything, I avoided spending long periods of time outside. It was too dangerous. I didn't interact with anyone inside the barracks. The following day, around noon, I spotted a few tank crewmen wandering through the square with dishes. I could smell not only warm food, but also an opportunity for me – I have a good nose for both! The crewmen were very young, a group of recently trained recruits who were leaving the barracks and were about to be thrown into battle. I thought to myself: 'They sure need an old hand like me. I should talk to them.' A short exchange took place between me and a *Gefreiter*:[6]

'Who are you?'

'We're coming back from the barracks. We were stopped because we are going to fight here.'

'What tanks do you have?'

'None at the moment. We have two Panthers and a Tiger in the workshop which are being repaired. We also have a few assault artillery guns – old training vehicles with short 75mm calibre barrels. There's no ammo for them, so they're going to reassemble them with 20mm anti-aircraft guns!'

It's not ideal, but it's still better than marching against the Russians with just a rifle. I went with the boys to report to the officer at the

6. Lance corporal.

cadet school and *Oberfeldwebel*[7] Sander, who was organising an armoured group in Poznań. Sander was about 30 years old, but he seemed athletic and spoke with an Austrian accent. However, he didn't give me any hope of getting into a tank. Over 100 people were 'acting' as infantry soldiers due to the lack of vehicles. He said: 'I just need a gunner for my Tiger and he must be trained to handle 88s!'[8] I showed him my military ID and driver's licence. When he noticed that I could drive as well as operate an 88, he quickly said: 'Alright, you're my man!'

Initially, the Tiger wasn't yet operational. During that time I stayed at Fort Rauch and worked as *Hauptmann*[9] Wolf von Malotki's messenger at the V Infantry Cadet School in Poznań. He was a swashbuckling soldier who was awarded the Knight's Cross, and was a commander of Armoured Shock Reserve at the time. During the first attack on the railway embankment undertaken by the infantry school's cadets on 27 January 1945, his vehicle was hit by an anti-tank gun. He was injured in the leg as a result, and shortly after was transported back to his homeland by plane. He wasn't there to witness what happened to the cadets, of which only a few hundred were taken prisoner.

Boredom bothered me. I set up an MG42[10] on a tripod in the square and shot at Soviet fighter planes[11] that flew over Poznań from time to time, although they never dropped any bombs. They looked like reconnaissance flights. In order not to reveal my location, I didn't use trace ammunition, but aside from that, I carried on scheming. On an empty farm I found five little piglets. A Polish fisherman killed four of them and provided me with a cold roast, which would become my

7. Sergeant Major.
8. 8,8 cm KwK 36 L/56 88mm calibre – the primary armament of a PzKpfw VI Tiger I tank.
9. Captain.
10. *Maschinengewehr 42* – popular German machine gun.
11. Iliuszyn Ił-2 or Ił-10.

main source of food for the next four weeks. Two barges were moored at the bank of the River Warta, each loaded with over 300 tonnes of sugar. This was where my nose failed me. I stumbled upon field gendarmery's post, who were also known as 'chained dogs'.[12] They threatened me: either I had to leave quickly or face a court martial. I disappeared!

12. Known as such due to their 'ryngraphs' that were carried on chains.

Chapter 2

Serious Situation

The streets were constantly filled with refugee convoys heading west. Families from the country, wagons loaded with beds and household goods, cars damaged with shrapnel, the injured, women and children – each with fear all over their faces. They were civilians fleeing Russians! Additionally, there were retreating army and artillery units which had been ordered to pull back further from the front. Should I run as well? This was probably the very first time I felt complete resignation, and bad feelings completely encircled me.

What was the overall situation? Initially, we had 10,000 people in Poznań, which left us with no chance when confronted with the powerful force of a Russian attack. Our main combat force consisted of around 1,300–1,500 cadets from the V Infantry School. The rest were *Landesschützen,*[13] police units, and *Volkssturm*. Poznań was declared a Festung (fortress) in order to increase its combat potential. In reality it meant 'Whoever left Festung Poznań would be punished in Germany!' Soldiers coming from the Eastern Front, vacationers from their home country, convalescents etc., all were detained and incorporated into the Festung's garrison. Nevertheless, even the experienced officers were hesitant to resist. The military commander in Poznań was General Mattern, a tall, well-built man, known as 'the father' to his soldiers and for his sense of humour. He jokingly tried to lift the men's spirits by saying: 'The situation will only be truly shitty when we can no longer help ourselves!' However, even

13. Territorial Guard.

to him, the defence of Poznań seemed impossible. He considered thrusting through to the west, but there were clear orders from the Fuhrer: 'Engage significant enemy forces through resistance'. Hitler and Himmler believed that as a major railway junction, Poznań was a significant target for the Russians and their supply lines. It was to be defended to the last man. Even later, when the train stations were already in the hands of the Russians, allowing them to transport their resources to the front without hindrance, the OKW refused to comply with the requests of Mattern and his second-in-command Gonell to break out of the Festung. At first, the Russians looked for weak spots in Poznań's defensive system, and German units also sent their patrols to assess the situation. The battle group consisting of cadets from the Infantry School, under the command of Major Schulte, and several assault guns and armoured vehicles, set off towards the south-east. Near Września, they unexpectedly stumbled upon Russian armoured vehicles, but managed to break away despite fire from the enemy tanks. Schulte's unit powered through and, despite suffering considerable losses, reached Poznań on 22 January 1945.

Chapter 3

Enter the Tiger

My first action was a reconnaissance mission around the outskirts of Poznań, and was made in cooperation with the Panther. Our crew was truly first-class. The commander was *Oberfeldwebel* Sander, who had experienced the Russian Front in 1941 and had destroyed around thirty-five destroyed tanks. Our driver was a Berliner, *Unteroffizier*[14] Heckmann, who, if you believed what he said, was supposedly 'unbreakable'. He would later be shot in 1947 in Karelia, 600 km from Leningrad. He hated captivity and, with three of his comrades, had tried to flee from the Karelian tundra, but a burst of machine gun fire ended their escape. The loader was Kurt Algner from Wrocław, who worked like he was on a remote control: he knew that MG by heart and I only witnessed his machine gun jam once. Our radio operator was Kirrmeier and I never ever heard him utter a word of objection. I myself remained a gunner.

***

We went past infantry soldiers laying in trenches. They directed our attention to a water tower 1 km away (in Swarzędz), where a Russian lookout had taken shelter and was guiding the artillery from. They responded to the slightest of movements with a series of shots. You couldn't even stick the tip of your finger out of the trenches. We watched and moved forward cautiously, the only sound in our

14. NCO

headphones being Sander's soft commands. Suddenly, the Russians spotted us. Through my viewfinder and side scope I could see a wave of dust and broken tree branches. The artillery had already fired on this street, so we turned right, into the area covered with trees and further ahead, on our right, was the Panther. Suddenly, we heard our commander's voice: 'Tower at two o'clock, distance 1,200, missile to the upper window of the water tower.'

As soon as the command was given, I rotated my tank turret, pushed the actuator pedal, and set my scope. I heard Algner's message: 'gun loaded!' and when ordered to 'fire!' I pulled the trigger. There was a boom, the gun moved backwards and the shell went through the window. The explosion blew away the roof, bricks fell, and a cloud of

A modern photograph of the water tower in Swarzędz. (*Rafał Jerzak*)

dust rose around the water tower. I hear Sander again: 'Delayed missile to the base of the tower!' The shell pierced the wall and exploded inside. Any potential lookout surely had to have been neutralised, but it was becoming dangerous for us, too. The fire intensified and in front of us we spotted two suspicious positions firing in our direction. The Russians had probably installed a few anti-tank guns. We received a signal from the Panther next to us: 'We've been hit again, we're immobilised, cover us!'

We moved in front of the Panther, trying to avoid exposing our side to the enemy. The crew got out and under enemy fire, tried to replace the caterpillar tracks. We were successful and the Panther began to retreat. When we also received the order to withdraw, the accelerator pedal didn't respond and the engine sat there idling away. The tank could neither move forwards nor backwards. Damn it! The gear lever must've been either broken or disconnected and so there was only one solution: get out and change gear manually. At that point, my armoured vehicle mechanic training came in handy and I prepared to exit the tank. We rotated the turret to six o'clock and while the Panther covered me, I climbed out through the hatch and lay flat against the armour plating. I could hear the sound of passing Russian shells, including the characteristic shots of dangerous infantry cannons[15]. When they were fired, you heard the shell even before the actual shot. With trembling hands, I lifted the engine's heavy cover, grabbed the lever and pushed. The motor was screaming in top gear. The Tiger practically jumped backwards and Heckmann let go of the clutch.

We left the danger zone and hid behind a house in order to repair the damages. We had succeeded once more and had survived our trial by fire.

15. Division Cannon 1942 (ZiS-3).

Chapter 4

'Ivan' Approaches from the South

Oberst[16] Gonell, who until then had been acting as the commander of the cadet school in Poznań, was a natural soldier. He mainly placed his Junkers in the eastern part of the city, where they anticipated the expected assault. The Russians had lost a significant number of tanks on the eastern side of the Festung in the first days of the fighting, yet still continued to conduct heavy attacks in that area. Now they attempted to attack the Festung from a different direction. They quickly managed to establish bridgeheads south of the city and, as a result, were able to redirect heavy weapons to the south and west of Poznań. After several previous and ineffective attacks, on 26 and 27 January they created a huge breakthrough in the Festung's southern defensive zone. Taking advantage of this success, they broke into the southern and south-western suburbs and drove the completely inexperienced Luftwaffe soldiers to the edge of downtown. The Germans then formed the so-called Old Grolman Bolt – Queen Jadwiga's Embankments (Burggrafen Ring) – between Fort Grolman and the River Warta.

The Panther, which was brought in to protect the Saint Roch Bridge, had been hit sixteen times by anti-tank guns, forcing the crew to flee the vehicle. We received an order to tow the Panther away from the Russian's zone of fire. The *Oberfeldwebel* of the Luftwaffe's field division guided me to the scene. His golden *Kampfspange* and numerous other decorations indicated that he was no novice.

16. Colonel.

We advanced forwards to help the stricken Panther and its crew. It was a dark night. Heckmann followed the blunt orders of the *Oberfeldwebel*, who stood next to me in the turret's open hatch. Everything around us was peaceful and quiet: not a single shot was fired. The Russians probably didn't believe we were going to recover the damaged tank.

We hooked the Panther up with two ropes and the crew climbed on board. The journey began. I tried to assess the area through the viewfinder, but without success. I suddenly saw a brief flash and two seconds later there was a horrible explosion. The whole turret was filled with a fountain of fire and all I could see all around me were flames. I thought I was going to suffocate. I wanted to scream, but couldn't get a single word out. On the contrary, every time I gasped for air I felt like my lungs were being torn apart.

We were now leaving the danger zone. Heckmann instinctively reacted as he should and put his foot down. When I turned on the

The PzKpfw V Panther destroyed on 27 January 1945 at ul. Górna Wilda, in the Wildecki Market Square. It was one of two tanks of this type that fought on the streets of Poznań in 1945. (*ZR*)

light I saw a disembodied arm and the *Oberfeldwebel*'s lower body behind me, which only a few moments before had been standing in the turret's open hatch.

The Russians cut off our retreat and tried to destroy us from the nearest basement window using a captured Panzerfaust. Thankfully, they only hit the hatch: had they hit 10cm lower, it would've been the end of us. The shockwave turned all the armoured glass into dust, which settled in my lungs and blocked any air from entering. Taking on a tank in a street fight is a complicated matter and certainly isn't as simple as it seems! We were afraid that our inexperienced soldiers would attack us with Panzerfausts from the basement windows. What's more, they may have been further confused by the fact that you hardly saw German tanks in Poznań. That's why we put a swastika flag we'd found earlier on the front of the Tiger. When they saw us, the Russians would probably have thought: 'They must be genuine fascists!' However, our only motivation for doing so was to make sure our own soldiers could identify us. Many of our comrades still remember it.

I was aware of the possible dangers our actions in Poznań might bring, so I stayed very vigilant. I didn't have much time to think, though. Heavy fighting in the south and west of Poznań required constant activity. 'Ivan' attacked us from every direction. We had to stop breakthroughs, repel any new attacks, destroy anti-tank weapons and chase away any Russian tanks that managed to get through. The Infantry's School cadets continued to set a great example to everyone. *Oberfeldwebel* Scholz was the first to destroy three T-34s with a Panzerfaust. The 173 destroyed Russian tanks testified to the huge amount of heavy armour used in Poznań. Directly behind the front line was the building of a former gynaecological clinic, which at the time was being used as the main dressing station. After only a few hours it was already full, and in the operating room patients were constantly being treated on multiple operating tables. The doctors had been working continuously for twelve, performing around

400 procedures a day. There was no point worrying about the last man in the queue. During the night, the clinic needed to be emptied as it was in such close proximity to the main front line. The wounded were moved out in cars and on stretchers to the Ostland Hotel.[17] The streets were under enemy fire and as the Russian guns had now started to reach the hotel, the building began to turn into a pile of rubble and so the dressing station was set up in the basement.

17. Now the Hotel Rzymski.

Chapter 5

From Floor to Floor

The anti-aircraft basements proved to be an obstacle in leading an effective defence of Poznań, because they legally required two exits. Usually, the second exit was a hole punched into a wall of the neighbouring house, allowing you to move easily between buildings. The Russians used this to their advantage. After breaking into one of the districts, after a while they'd appear in a completely different place, sometimes even in the middle of the city, as they waded through the basements full of terrified Poles. As a result, we had to give up defending individual buildings. Often, while our soldiers were fighting on the upper floors or even the ground floor, the Russians were already in the basement. Those who refused to give up ended up being blown up. During the fighting, we constantly felt the lack of heavy weapons and sufficient anti-aircraft defensive systems. The planes used by Russians – both modern, fast American bombers as well as outdated Russian machines – systematically shot and bombed German positions day and night.

The enemy started to penetrate the defensive systems in the southern part of the city and we were called in to secure one of the intersections. It was suspiciously quiet all around. Behind us, there were Germans in houses and in front of us: 'no-man's land'. We stopped in front of an advertising post in the very centre of the intersection; a field of fire stretching out along the two streets. We turned off the engine so as not to reveal ourselves, but this nearly brought us great misfortune. We observed the neighbourhood: apart from the regular rifle and artillery fire, everything seemed calm. There was nothing out of the ordinary. Were we where we were supposed to be? We kept watching, without moving. We thought about shooting the windows of the surrounding houses with our MG, but then spotted around fifteen 'Ivans' jumping over a pile of rubble and hiding behind a wall. They peaked out from around the corner, but still we didn't move. Maybe they thought the tank had been abandoned? Suddenly, after ten minutes of no action, machine gun fire was directed at us and, at the same time, I heard our commander's voice: 'T-34 at 6 o'clock, distance 450m, armour-piercing missile.' Our engine was still off so I started screaming 'Heckmann, go! Go!' Along with Sander, we manually turned the turret to the left. The Russian tank was now behind us and started to appear from behind the wall of the house. Its turret began to turn and target us. Our engine kicked in and I pushed the actuator's pedal, turning the turret counter-clockwise. Fractures of seconds decided everything. I pressed my eye to the scope, my hand on the trigger. I could see the tank's rear: 'Now!' Boom! Yet at the same time as our gun fired, I also saw the flash from the T-34 as well. They missed! My shell hit their 'bathtub',[18] causing plumes of smoke. Another shot. The T-34 exploded almost simultaneously with the sound of the gun firing. Later, I noticed that their shell had obliterated the advertising pole behind us. 'Ivan' obviously had weaker nerves than us, that's why he missed. We'd stopped the breakthrough. It was a huge relief for us, but once again our lives were hanging in the balance. We were all terrified and so no one said a word as we made our way back.

During the ride I kept looking through the viewfinder. I saw deserted houses with German soldiers standing in their entrances, who waved at us as we passed. At the next intersection we passed a truck full of Russians. Sander shouted: 'MG, fire!' I had the truck perfectly in the middle of my scope and expected to riddle it full of bullet holes. I pulled the trigger, but nothing happened! The rifle was jammed and the truck drove past us. I heard Sander exhale loudly. At the last possible moment, we realised it wasn't a truck full of Russians, but the Hungarian unit which fought alongside us in Poznań to the very end. The soldiers wore brown uniforms very similar to the Russian ones. It was a miracle.

---

18. Common name for the main body of a tank.

Chapter 6

Change of Command

The streets were under heavy fire from Russian artillery and shell fire. We were under constant air raids, mainly from Russian bombers which, due to the lack of any anti-aircraft defences, had no obstacles in their way. The situation kept getting worse.

On 28 January, even General Mattern admitted on a radio-telegram:

'The situation within the Festung has definitely worsened! Despite their heroism, the *Landeschützen*, *Standorttruppen* and *Luftwaffe* units no longer have decisive combat value! The troops are yielding under enemy fire and the onslaught of enemy tanks. I ask for relief from the outside.'

The next day, Poznań reported again:

'Heavy street fighting in the southern and western parts of the city. The constant fire from guns and mortars is directed on our positions. There are over 2,000 wounded in military hospitals at the moment. Over 600 of them need to be evacuated immediately. Transport is only possible by air. The last landing site is under enemy fire. I'm asking for two battalions of paratroopers to secure it.'

Thanks to these radio messages, the soldier's 'father' wasn't very well liked by his superiors. Two days later, on 30 January, General Mattern received the following radio-telegram from *Reichsführer* SS Heinrich Himmler of the Army Group Vistula:

'To the commander of Festung Poznań! Due to combat experience and the fact that Festung Poznań will soon face heavy fighting, *Oberst* Gonell is appointed new commander of the Festung. General Mattern will pass over command to *Oberst* Gonell. I expect he will do so, regardless of his own beliefs.'

Only a few days later, Gonell was appointed major general. He had once been severely injured and even had a silver plate in his head, but this didn't stop him from serving. Until then, Gonell had been a commander of the 'Wschód' section, now, as the Festung commander, he moved into the Citadel, which was located on a hill, above the Garbary train station. There, on one of the underground floors, was the command post of the Festung commander. When Gonell took over, the southern and western suburbs were almost entirely in Russian hands. Around 10 February, we received the order to leave the military hospital in the basement of the Ostland Hotel. We moved to the slaughterhouse and the houses in front of the northern embankment of the Citadel, near Szelągowska Street (Raifeisenalle). We were once again suffering losses as the approach of the Russians forced us to transport the wounded once again. At first, Gonell didn't allow them to be placed in the Citadel, but when he finally agreed, the road from the slaughterhouse was already under constant enemy fire. Only fifty of the wounded, along with the medical personnel, managed to survive the evacuation. On 2 February, the Poznań Castle, full of wounded, fell into enemy hands. The fact that we still held Poznań itself was a testament to the Junkers at the cadet school who were appointed as *Leutnants*.[19]

19. Second Lieutenants.

Chapter 7

Run or Keep Fighting?

The Polish civilians, who sat in anti-aircraft basements, constantly watching the situation unfold, created a reconnaissance bridge for Russians. Every newly established facility was immediately shelled. An 'Acht Komma Acht'[20] installed in the square in front of the Castle was destroyed after a short while by 'Stalin's Organs.'[21]

Heckmann, Algner and I carried out a brief reconnaissance by the Warta River, aiming to investigate potential escape routes. The next day, we told Sander about our concerns: if the Russians keep strengthening their ring around Poznań, any escape attempt would be doomed. Did nobody understand this? The front had now reached the Oder River and any further hanging around would only result in getting trapped. However, Sander managed to dispel my doubts once again. He refused to believe that we were going to be left on our own and that help would eventually arrive from the outside. In his opinion, we would successfully break out of the Festung with the help of 1,300 cadets from the Infantry School, who so far had fought heroically. It was hard to doubt him, especially when he started to talk about heroism:

'You're an honest man!'

'You're already convinced about that?'

'Exactly, so you wouldn't run away leaving thousands of wounded comrades here, would you? You're one of the very few able to face the Russian tanks!'

---

20. 8,8 cm Flak 31 cal. 88 mm anti-aircraft cannon, often used as armour-piercing weapon.
21. BM-13 Katiusha Rocket Launchers.

'All right, I am honest, even when it turns out to be completely useless.'

Surely, even Sander would have looked at it differently if he any idea of what was in store. If only he knew he was about to be wounded and then blown up.

Apart from my Tiger, two Panthers, a Hetzer,[22] Panzer IV,[23] and Panzerhaubitz[24] with a 105 mm calibre cannon, there were probably no other German armoured vehicles in Poznań. What's more, all of these weapons were operating in different parts of the city. There were still a small number of assault guns, but they weren't sufficiently armed or fully functional as they had previously been used as training vehicles.[25] All of this meant that I stayed inside the Tiger for days. Loading the ammo and refuelling happened at night, with ammo and petrol being delivered by the *Sturmgeschütze*.

One evening, I was called to the vicinity of a railway bridge as behind it was a Russian assault gun. I scouted the area with my binoculars: the distance was 600m. We hid the tank behind a fence surrounding a garden. It was pitch black, so I turned on the backlight. Unfortunately, it was so dark that I couldn't see the enemy, besides, the fence was blocking my view. Sander was in the commander's position and being a bit higher than me, had a better field of view. I was just about to ram the fence when he said he would guide me to try and obtain a direct hit. I aimed between the fourth and fifth plank of the fence on the left, 2cm above the crossbeam. It should work. The command came: 'Fire!' The shell left the barrel and a few seconds later bursts of flames could be seen under the bridge. The

22. Self-propelled gun Jagdpanzer 38 (T) Hetzer (Tank destroyer).
23. Medium tank PzKpfw IV.
24. Most probably a SdKfz 142/2 – 10,5 Sturmhaubitze 42 self-propelled gun (Sturmgeschütz armed with a 105 mm calibre howitzer).
25. The author meant the vehicles used by the 500th Training-Reserve Assault Weapons Batallion, a unit with its barracks in Golęcin, near Poznań.

enemy vehicle had been hit on the first attempt and was now on fire. We retreated as quietly as possible so as not to expose ourselves.

***

The game of hide-and-seek continued. The Russians built a barricade near a tall building and hid an anti-tank gun behind it. Using the old-fashioned method, we moved on foot towards the intersection to discover the barricade had reached the second floor. Through the binoculars we spotted two anti-tank guns on the left and right. It would be dangerous if it turned out that 'Ivan' was in position, which was highly likely. A 76.5mm calibre gun could pierce the side of our tank from 500m away, so we could only show the front of the vehicle to the enemy. Having memorised all the necessary details, I withdrew.

The crew of the ZiS-3 anti-tank gun preparing to take up combat position during the street fighting in Poznań. (*Soviet newsreel*)

We prepared the Tiger for battle. The barrel was loaded with a high-explosive shell, while Algner kept other shells close at hand. My right hand was on the trigger as we drove up and shot from behind the corner. Halt! The first shell flew out and tore the cover off the gun to the left of the barricade. Algner was already loading the second shell – the finisher! We turned our turret to 1 o'clock. Suddenly, something exploded dangerously close by, right in front of us. The Russians had started firing from the second gun. I had them in my sight, fired, and hit the target. It was impossible to see any movement in the cloud of smoke and dust. Suddenly, Sander's voice: 'anti-tank!' We fired two shells and eventually the guns were destroyed. 'Driver, onwards!' We rammed through the barricade at full speed as the piles of wardrobes, carts, planks and other rubbish were launched into the air. Another ZiS-3 was there in the background. I rotated the turret and set the gun to a shot of 30m. I wiped the Russian gun off the face of the earth with our 'eighty-eight.' Its crew sat there with petrified faces. The commander's voice was heard again: 'Mission complete, reverse gear, quick march!'

Chapter 8

Losing Our Commander

It was supposed to be the last mission with our proven commander: Sander. During an enemy breakthrough, Sander took control of the Panzer IV with the intention of counterattacking. Time and again he fired at the running Russians. The 7.5 calibre gun's brake fluids heated up to near boiling point, which made the retractor less effective and the gun rocked back strongly after each shot. However, the Russians

In the foreground is the PzKpfw IV in which *Oberfeldwebel* Sander – the Tiger commander – was wounded. Behind it is a StuG III. The photograph was taken at the Citadel, after the battle. (*Soviet newsreel*)

continued to push forward and Sander was forced to keep firing. In just a short time, the tank fired seventy-five high-explosive shells and eventually the attack was stopped. The battle was nearing its end, but then Sander was wounded and taken to the Citadel with a crushed thigh. Over 1,000 wounded soldiers were already there, with beds spread out over four stories. Their fates hung in the balance.

***

By 25 January 1945 we were completely cut off. 'Ivan' kept coming and surrounded Poznań with a 7 km-wide ring. What's more, the front had now reached the Oder River, around 160 km to the west. Poznań was doomed. The most unbelievable rumours started spreading among the soldiers, possibly on purpose in order to motivate them to continue fighting and silence any thoughts of escape. Himmler sent a radio-telegram to Poznań on 28 January 1945: 'Hold on for another seven days. An armoured corps is coming from Zbąszynek to free you.'

No one knew if this was true or just another lie, but we carried on, regardless.

Our Tiger's crew now consisted of just three people: Heckmann – driver, Kurt Algner – loader, and finally me – gunner and commander.[26] We found three red Turkish hats (fez) in the uniform store, which also served as a mask rental shop. They perfectly matched our oil-stained faces and although I think we probably looked ridiculous, completely unlike any German soldiers, it was a way to keep our dark humour alive.

***

By the end of January, the Tiger was operating in the area around the Castle, where approximately 2,000 wounded were being treated.

26. In the meantime, the Tiger's radio operator, Kirrmeier, had been wounded due to artillery fire.

Russian infantry during the fighting in the area around the Citadel. (*Soviet newsreel*)

Opposite, at the entrance to one of the houses, a group of minesweepers were assigned to us for protection. I think it was 2 February, as we were exchanging a few cans of pork between us, that a messenger arrived with an order that the Tiger's commander must report immediately to SS *Obersturmbannführer*[27] Lenzer. The messenger looked at me with surprise when I picked up my Turkish hat as we are headed to the shelter.

In front of me I saw an exhausted and unshaven man lying on a wooden bench. Before him were two ringing telephones, which he answered from time to time. He gave me the following order: 'Four Russian tanks are in the middle of the castle bridge. See what you can do about it!'

27. Lieutenant Colonel.

Chapter 9

Four T-34s in One Go

We climbed up the basement stairs, grabbing some binoculars on the way and headed towards the Castle. Finally, we laid down on the ground and crawled the last 150 metres. When I peeked around the corner, I couldn't believe my own eyes: four T-34s[28] were standing quietly side by side. Their crews and several other soldiers were stood around them smoking cigarettes. Oh, I really wanted to show them! We crawled back the same way we'd come and when we'd nearly reached the Tiger, we met two medics carrying a wounded soldier on a stretcher:

'Hey, where are you guys going?'

'To the Castle, obviously!'

'In that case, wait 10 minutes and then you can go!' said Heckmann, 'Unless you want those four T-34s on the bridge to send you straight to the field hospital! If so, you're free to go right now!'

Both medics looked at us in surprise as we approached the minesweepers and discussed the plan of action. Immediately after, we climbed on board the tank and I set my turret to 9 o'clock. Heckmann had received precise instructions: we had to destroy all four tanks before any of them had the chance to fire. We had to succeed! None of them was allowed to escape. The minesweepers kicked up a bit of a fuss by firing their submachine guns and rifles in order to distract the Russians. Heckmann started the engine and the tank moved forward slowly. I pressed my eye to my viewfinder and could see the Castle walls.

---

28. In reality, at least two of them were IS-2 (Josef Stalin-2) heavy tanks.

Heckmann slowed down even more. We reached the corner: only 10 cm more. I squeezed the gun's dials with both hands, my visibility improving all the time. Not more than a quarter second later I had the last Russian tank in my sights. My shot coincided perfectly with driver's 'stop' and pierced through the T-34's body. The tank caught fire and its hatch started to open, but I didn't have time to focus on that as I immediately turned my gun and aimed for the second tank. I pulled the trigger, but once again I couldn't see the exact result of the hit, although I heard Algner's voice in my headphones: 'It's on fire! It's burning!' The third 'Ivan' was already in my scope and I fired with the same result as previous two. I start aiming for the foremost tank and the shell ripped through its side before it could fire a shot. After this, we retreated at full throttle to hide. It had all been as if we were on a

Above and opposite: The intersection of Aleja Marszałka Piłsudksiego (Tiergartenstrasse), currently ul. Zwierzyniecka and Aleja Marszałka Focha (Glogauerstrasse), currently ul. Roosevelt. The visible wrecks of the IS-2 tanks are two of the four Russian tanks destroyed by the Tiger on the western side of Kaponierra in January and February 1945. (*Zbigniew Grzegorski*)

shooting range. At a short distance of 450 metres, my 'eighty eight' could pierce through any armour the Soviet tanks had, especially when the 'bathtub' was hit: it's every tank's weakest spot.

We received a bottle of punch from Lenzer as a reward for our successful mission. I was very thirsty after eating pork and so took a great big sip, emptying nearly half of the bottle. Lenzer probably worried that I wouldn't be able to aim at anything after that, but Heckmann said: 'Don't you worry, *Obersturmbannführer*. Thanks to this water this boy will be able to shoot a hair off your bald head from 1,200 metres. Right?' For almost three weeks we'd been eating cured pork and rum, which helped with digestion, but at least this weak punch quenched our thirst.

***

After operating continuously throughout the day, then refuelling and replenishing ammunition at night, not to mention sleeping in the tank, we were so exhausted that we decided to spend at least one night in the Credit Zemstvo[29] building. I asked the mechanics to go and fix the rotation cylinder on the Tiger's turret as by then it could only be turned by hand, which was naturally a slow and tiresome process. We had to sleep on the floor and cover ourselves with mattresses. It wasn't the most comfortable, but at least I could stretch my legs and I was soon sound asleep. At dawn, I leapt to my feet after dreaming that the tank had been hit by a shell. I didn't know what was happening. I knew I wasn't asleep anymore but I could still hear the shots in quick succession and felt the walls of the building tremble. Through the windows I could see bricks falling down from the roof. The Soviet anti-tank gun thought it'd be funny to wake us up by firing

29. The *Ziemstwo Kredytowe* building (also known as the 'Gauhaus' during the Nazi occupation) was the headquarters of Arthur Greiser, the Reich Governor of Wartheland.

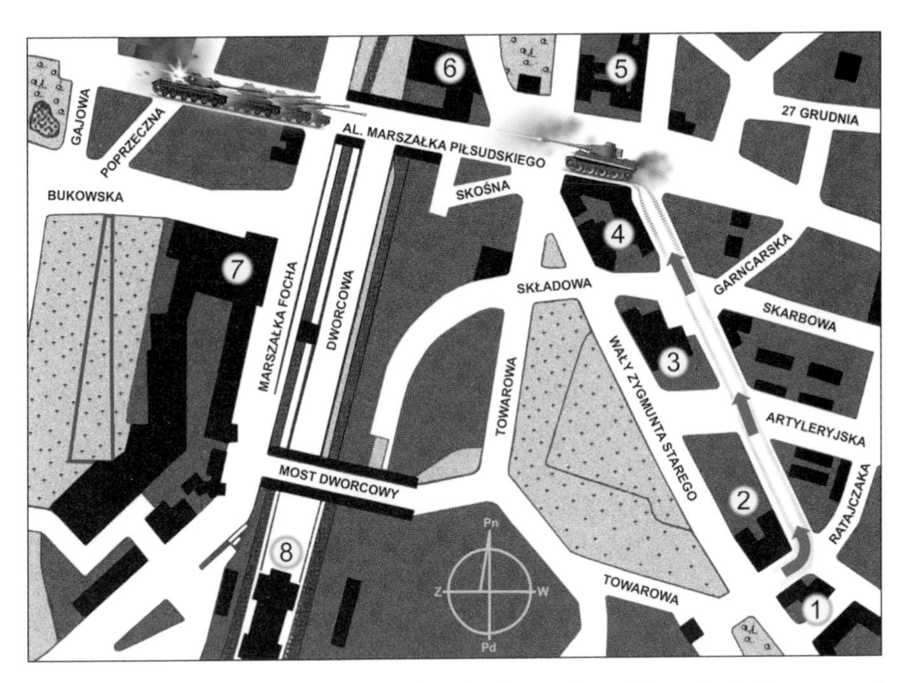

The route the Tiger took when destroying the four tanks at Kaponier in January and February 1945.

1. Soldier's House
2. Chamber of Crafts
3. Railway Directorate
4. Credit Zemstvo building
5. Citadel
6. University
7. Poznań Fair
8. Main Railway Station

at us from the nearby park as shell after shell struck the building's upper floors. Despite the other soldiers' protests, who were no doubt worried that the Russians would target our window next, I took the MG 42 and moved towards it. After the first round, the Russians were hiding behind an anti-aircraft bunker and the shelling ceased. When any of them tried to stick their nose out, my blue 'beans' whizzed past their ears.

One time, I saw a T-34 and a large self-propelled gun with a huge barrel[30] go along the road by the Credit Zemstvo. The Tiger was parked right in the middle of the square and I prayed they wouldn't notice

30. Most likely an ISU-152 or ISU-122.

it. I'd never ran down the stairs as fast as I did then! The only person I could find under the mattresses to join me was Fred Heckmann. Some unknown tank crewman appeared next to us and yelled: 'I'll be your loader!' He was an *Obergefreiter* from Saxony and was later promoted to *Unterofficier* for showing exceptional heroism in the face of the enemy. We jumped into the Tiger, the engine was wailing and I turned my turret. Before reached open ground, I noticed a few Russians pushing a heavy machine gun mounted on a sled. I aimed quickly and pulled the trigger: the shell wiped the sledge clean away. As we came around the corner, we spotted two Russians: 'Driver, stop!' The distance was around 400 metres and we wanted to take care of the first, so that the other couldn't run away. Aim, load and fire, no unnecessary commands, just like on a shooting range. The projectile left the barrel and all I could see were branches falling from the surrounding trees following the shockwave. But what was

The remains of the Credit Zemstovo building. During the war it served as the headquarters for Arthur Greiser, Reich Governor of Wartheland. (*Zbigniew Grzegorski*)

going on!? My scope had fogged up! The *Obergefreiter* shouted: 'Come on! Come on! Fire! The assault gun is turning!' But I still couldn't see anything. Just in case, I fired again without aiming. Then, my visibility returned and I saw that the T-34 in front of us was on fire and the assault gun was trying to turn around in the street. But I was faster! My missile bit into its rear and smoke started to appear from the vehicle, but it still kept trying to turn left. I aimed again and fired into its side to finish it off. Finally! The giant exploded. 'Reverse gear, move!' and we cautiously retreated. Now I wanted to take care of the anti-tank gun that had woken us so rudely that morning. However, there wasn't enough space as the Tiger was too low, so we drove up the street on the other side to get closer to them. Five high-explosive shells got the job done and we returned to the square to get some more respite in the Credit Zemstvo building. Our rest had prevented a very unpleasant situation from happening.

Chapter 10

Near the Chamber of Crafts

During the first days of February, the Chamber of Crafts, just like the Castle square, the university and the old Grolman Fort, was one of the most fiercely defended bastions. The resistance point changed hands four times. As soon as the Junkers captured the building and handed it over to the police and territorial units to defend, the Russians attacked it again and stormed the facility. The Chamber of Crafts, where 'Ivan' had settled, needed to be captured once again.

Through my viewfinder, I watched the Russians firing and throwing grenades from the basement windows. They weren't any threat to us like this. According to reports from our scouts, 'Ivan' had dug in and expanded his positions behind the Chamber. We wanted to make their stay in those holes as miserable as we could. I ordered a demolition shell with a delayed fuse to be loaded, so when I fired it it bounced off the ground around 100 metres from their positions. This meant the shell would fly flat about 1 metre off the ground and then explode after 50-100 metres. Taking into account the impact of shrapnel and the blast range of the 88, its effects can be pretty predictable.

Shot after shot was fired. We moved closer in order to shoot from as close a position as possible. The Russians were firing at us from barracks about a kilometre ahead. Suddenly, Algner looked to our right and started screaming: 'Oh God, there's an anti-tank gun on our right! Turret to 9 o'clock, now!' Turning the crank like a madman, I noticed Algner was helping me by turning his commander's crank as well. My eye was pressed to the scope and that's when I saw a

The fight for the Chamber of Crafts - a frame taken from a Russian film. (*Soviet newsreel*)

92 mm anti-tank gun[31] on a tow truck. Thankfully, it was aimed in the opposite direction, but eight or nine Russians were busy turning it towards us. However, my missile was already waiting in the barrel and the stream of fire was about 10 metres long. I couldn't see what was going on due to all the dust and smoke. Just to make sure, I fired again without changing the setting. Looking through the machine gun's optics, I continued to fire using the pedal.

31. In fact, the 92 mm was never used by the Red Army. There was a rumour among German soldiers that the Russians had acquired new, modern anti-tank guns of this calibre. Hence the author, when speaking about 76.2 mm guns, mistook them for being 92 mm guns.

As the dust settled and the smoke began to clear, we could see a mountain of scrap metal which a few moments earlier had been the anti-tank gun. Further fire was unnecessary in this situation. It could have been the reverse. The Soviet 92 mm gun was the newest and most efficient anti-tank weapon and could easily penetrate the Tiger's armour, especially on its side. The disadvantage of classic guns, however, is that the barrel only turned about 30° to the left and right, meaning it needed to be directed at the target, otherwise the entire thing had to be turned. In this case, a tank with a rotating turret was obviously much faster.

Soon after, the Junkers came and scared 'Ivan' out of his hiding place and the Chamber of Crafts was once again under our control. But the Russians didn't give up that easily and kept firing at the Junkers from their barracks a kilometre away.

I kept firing high-explosive shells until their resistance collapsed. We were still on standby when suddenly, right in front of us next to the tower, there was a massive explosion that shook the entire tank: 'Damn it! Tell me they didn't bring another anti-tank gun?'

After a quick look-around I shouted: 'There!' There was a second hit and I heard Algner's voice in my headphones: 'Retreat! Quickly!' Before we'd managed to withdraw and hide behind the corner, we were hit twice. We assessed the damage from behind the Chamber of Crafts: four fist-sized holes near the turret yoke cover. They looked like they'd been cut out of the armoured plate. The Russians were shooting quite well, but fortunately for us, they'd hit our most armoured spot. They'd probably wanted to hit us near the turret's ring, one of the most vulnerable spots in every tank. Such a hit could tear away the whole turret, or at least immobilise the turning mechanism. After our retreat, the Russian anti-tank gun kept firing but the Junkers were unable to locate its position. We assumed it must have been a Russian tank trying to neutralise us, but not having succeeded, had gone back into hiding. We waited, ready, but nothing else was going to happen that night.

The Chamber of Crafts following the battle. The wreckage of the T-34/85 tank is visible on the left. (*Zbigniew Grzegorski*)

The next afternoon, a 'tank' alarm was set off in our immediate vicinity. Nearby, I heard caterpillars crunching and engines whirring. Infantry soldiers directed us to the district under our control. We drove along the side street and stopped just before the intersection. There were Russians on the right, just beyond the intersection, so I kept an eye on this area. Our gun was loaded with an anti-tank missile, I set the firing distance to 450 metres, kept my hand on the trigger, and pressed my eye to the scope. Just let 'Ivan' show himself! Suddenly, we saw two small tanks: 'flamethrowers'.[32]As they passed, they launched jets of fire left and right. I took my aim and heard the gunshot boom: 'missed!' Impossible! The second shot missed the target as well. This couldn't be happening. I could always rely on my intuition. I shot twice more in their direction, but with no result and the Russian tanks left our sight. We all fell silent. Finally, Heckmann said: 'Man, it could've been a firework display!' We fell back to hide. I felt as though I could see the scorn in our infantry soldiers' eyes. I daren't approach them. Something must have happened to the gun. We decided to go to Citadel to ask someone to assess the damage. The scope, as it turned out, had shifted as a result of the four hits we'd suffered the previous day. Later that night, while we went looking for alternative accommodation, the mechanics were able to recalibrate the viewfinder.

32. They could have been OT-130s (T-26 light tank equipped with a flamethrower), but were more likely OT-34s, ie T-34/76 medium tanks with flamethrowers.

Chapter 11

At the Citadel

What was the situation at the Citadel – over 100 years old and our fortified headquarters – at the time? The building was surrounded by brick walls, covered on the outside with earth, with an open square in the centre. Underground corridors connecting some of the buildings were filled with the wounded. It was like an anthill: there wasn't an inch of free space on the ground for us to stretch our bones. Not only was it the main rendezvous point for the fighting units, but also a supply depot, with a bakery and kitchen on the lowest floors. The Citadel was under constant enemy fire as the Russians had realised long before how important it was. In a room with two windows looking out onto the square, I squeezed myself between the soldiers who were laying on the floor like sardines in a tin. While many of the wounded tried to carry on fighting with what little strength they had left, others hid in the basement. Nobody wanted to get hurt and die a slow death in a stronghold surrounded by Russians. Ammunition, food and medical supplies were delivered by air via parachute drops.

I lay down on some straw to try and get some sleep, but it was impossible in such a damp and stuffy room. There were a few Hindenburg lamps in the middle of the room, but not enough to provide any decent light. Russian 'sewing machines'[33] constantly flew over the Citadel dropping bombs, encountering no resistance from anti-aircraft artillery. The Russians used spotlights to send signals to

33. Soviet multi-purpose Polikarpow Po-2 aircraft.

each other, and the brick walls trembled under the bombs as if they had a fever.

A brief wailing was heard followed by a massive explosion. Brick dust and smoke suffocated me. The other soldiers jumped up scared and started running towards the door trying to get outside. Thankfully, I was laying by the wall, otherwise I would have been trampled to death. The artillery shell had hit right between the windows.

The Tiger was almost a casualty of this attack as well. A series of volley fire from 'Stalin's Organs' had reached it and it was now on fire. Despite ongoing artillery fire, a brave tankman ran towards the vehicle and dowsed the flames with a fire extinguisher. Then, he started the engine and drove out of the firing zone at full speed. Unfortunately, he couldn't operate the 7-speed gearbox and pushed the tank so much that he damaged the clutch. The tank was immobilised: our best anti-tank weapon was now unable to be driven. The heroic tankman, *Obergefreiter* Fischer, was the very same one who'd helped me as a loader during the Credit Zemstvo mission, back when we defeated two Russian tanks. He'd proved himself to be a genuine Saxon.

Sometime later, he proved his exceptional courage one again and, as a reward, was promoted to *Unteroffizier.* It happened after an aerial bomb had penetrated all four floors of the Redoubt Barracks and landed, without exploding, in a bakery full of *Landsers*. As the panicked soldiers started to flee, nearly trampling each other to death, Fischer calmly picked up the bomb and carried it outside. Luckily, the bomb didn't explode. It could've been a dud, or a time bomb.

There were still about 500-800 soldiers and *Leutnants*[34] in the combat zone on the eastern bank of the Warta, as well as a large

34. The author meant Leutnants and Oberleutnants from the V Infantry Cadet School

Above and below: The bombing of the Citadel. Explosions can be seen in the area of Ravelin II, on the opposite side of the Redit Koszarowa. (*Soviet newsreel*)

number of wounded in the 'Nivea'[35] factory and the school for the deaf. By 15 February, they were packed into such a small area that their end the following day was easily predictable. Only a few were able to break through to the Citadel as the final city bridge was already in enemy hands, and the railway bridge to the north-east of the cathedral had been blown up. On the night of 15/16 February, a long column of soldiers and wounded started their march after being granted permission by the commanders to break out of the eastern bridgehead. Approximately 800-1,200 men, led by *Leutnant* Nölke,[36] former commander of the Armoured Shock Reserve, broke through somewhere in the north-east, next to Fort Hake (Nölke, obeying an order, had previously searched for the best place to breach). There was complete calm among the Russian outposts. Without a word or even the slightest rustle, the column of 'ghosts' made its way silently and secretly through the night and the snowy fields. It wasn't until the next day that the Russians noticed the German positions in front of them were already empty. What had seemed impossible was now a fact: around 1,000 people had broken free from their death grip and through the Soviet circle surrounding Poznań. But this was only the beginning of an act of despair: having passed the Russians, the soldiers then split into smaller groups and tried to reach the German lines in Pomerania. Only a few hundred of them would make it.

Meanwhile, back in Poznań, the only ongoing fighting took place around the Citadel. The majority of the resistance points in the city and the outside forts had been abandoned, while others had been cut off and left on their own, fighting to the bitter end. Major General Gonell broadcast the following radio-telegram to Himmler:

---

35. Currently the Beiersdorf-Lechia S.A. factory at Gnieźnieńska 32.
36. Leutnant Hans Nölke commanded the advance guard of the group that broke out of the stronghold's eastern section. The overall commanders of the group were Major Hahn and Major Shulte.

The ruins of the Redita barracks at the Citadel. (*Michał Mucha*)

'The enemy is systematically destroying house after house, and the outposts are then fired with 'flamethrowers' by the infantry.'

The last free entrance of the Citadel was the North Gate. With help from the Sturmgeschütz, my Tiger was dragged through the gate and then well-hidden at the edge of a nearby forest. Its task was to guard and keep the road enemy-free. I could see the vast expanse of the Zeppelin Meadow[37] in front of me and a huge hangar to the left. It was a great position for me: I had a free field of fire within a 180° radius, meaning the Russians were forced to pass through this open space. It all made me very happy. There was a house 30 metres ahead of the Tiger and we occupied three quarters of it. Aside from Polish civilians, there was also a group of German infantrymen sheltering there. We occupied the second floor, from which we had

37. Also known as the Zeppelinwiese, it was a German airfield during the Battle for Poznań.

a perfect vantage point. One of us was constantly sat there all the time watching the Russians' movements. In case of an alarm, we only needed a few seconds to run through the trenches to reach the Tiger and climb on board.

***

Our supplies had improved as well. We were closer to the source and for the first time in four weeks we had warm soup. It was delicious! However, I was still worried about my health. It was so cold in the tank at night and my throat was so sore that I could hardly swallow anything, and on top of that, I also had a fever. I decided to try to find a doctor in the Citadel, but my efforts were in vain: thousands of wounded soldiers lay unattended on cramped bunkbeds, waiting for medical attention. Many of them didn't make it and died from their wounds. The doctors were operating continuously, day and night, but

A contemporary photograph of the house at Aleja Za Cytadelą (Steuben Allee), currently ul. Za Cytadelą, where the Tiger's crew were quartered. (*Maciej Karalus*)

were unable to keep up with the waves of wounded. It didn't take long for painkillers and bandages to run out. The atmosphere in those underground corridors was filled with screams and groans of the wounded. I left the Citadel almost in a hurry, resolving to search the neighbouring houses for first-aid kits. In a mansion that probably belonged to some high-ranking head of the Labour Service, at least judging by the size of the library, I managed to find a medicine cabinet. I swallowed a handful of strep throat lozenges on the spot, and took with me anything I thought might come in handy later.

***

During the day, we reported our observations to Gonell in the command bunker. We took it in turns with Heckmann, while Algner took care of us by staying in the basement and acting as our cook. The daily commute to make our report certainly wasn't easy. There was constant enemy fire as Russian snipers in neighbouring houses controlled the entire area. Only after dusk, while intermittently hiding, could you run in the road.

On 8 February, my birthday (I was 23), I paid our injured commander *Oberfeldwebel* Sander a visit. For destroying my tenth tank and even more heavy anti-tank guns, I'd been promoted to *Unteroffizier* and presented with a bottle of champagne. At the time, the latter was the most important to me. Sander was laying on his bunk, encapsulated in a cast up to his stomach, but still hoping to get out of there. He simply refused to believe that the German command would abandon us and was still confident that outside help would arrive. Thankfully, he didn't know what future was in store for him and other wounded in the Citadel. I myself had a strange feeling that this was the end and the situation was hopeless, but we kept fighting.

One morning, an observer in the attic spotted a T-34 tank on the edge of the Zeppelin Meadow. Sound the alarm! We sneaked up through a roadside trench and boarded the Tiger. Our driver, Fred Heckmann, took over as commander and watched the foreground through binoculars. Kurt Algner loaded the gun: 'Distance 1,200, fire!' I put my eye to the viewfinder. I'd been targeting the T-34 for a long time, but delayed my shot. The Russian tank was dead ahead so I hoped it would soon turn around to expose its side. It slowly started moving and Heckmann, apparently worried of losing sight of it, shouted: 'Fire! Fire! You'll let them get away, man!' Don't you worry, I'll get them. The enemy approached and turned slowly, hesitantly exposing its side. Just a little bit more! Perfect – the roar of the shot and my shell hit the bathtub! The T-34 was on fire! We didn't risk exposing our position by firing any further shots and so headed home to watch the action from there.

After sitting in the attic for a short while, the air raid alarm sounded. Sliding down the handrail, we headed down to the basement. The Russians were attacking using twin-engine American bombers that fired rockets at ground facilities. The long whistle of the rockets from a low height had a very depressing and nerve-wracking effect on us. 'Ivan' dropped a whole load of incendiary bombs nearby, two of which pierced through the roof and hit the floor. We probably wouldn't have even noticed if it wasn't for the Polish owner of the house (who'd fled to the attic after hearing the rockets) bringing it to our attention. Together, we extinguished the phosphorus with sand prepared for such an occasion.

An even bigger group of tankmen lived in the house next door and it was here I met the *Gefreiter* whom I'd previously accosted in the minesweepers' barracks and who was responsible for helping me join the Tiger's crew. His name was Alfred Leupold and he came from Hof, in Oberfranken. He'd been fighting in the outskirts of Poznań as a member of a Hetzer crew (a self-propelled gun manufactured in the Skoda factory). When I mentioned the patrol that we were planning to carry out that night in order to investigate potential escape routes, he was eager to join us. We set off: my loader Kurt Algner, Gefreiter Fred Leupold and me. The road to the Warta was still clear and we walked along the riverbank without encountering any obstacles or the

The PzKpfw VI Tiger standing on Aleja Za Cytadelą (Steuben Allee), next to the house where its crew was quartered, and from where it fired towards the Zeppelin Meadow. (*Soviet newsreel*)

enemy himself. After about 3 kilometres we decided to head back. Further reconnaissance was pointless: any attempt to escape always relied on the circumstances at the time. We only wanted to familiarise ourselves with the area closest to our positions. When we returned to the basement wet and dirty, a *Wachtmeister*[38] from the '500' unit said:

'Where have you been?'

'We were reconnoitring the River Warta.'

'You wanna escape, huh? Haven't you sworn to the Führer? Remember: whoever leaves their post here in Poznań will immediately be court-martialled. I'll order him to be hanged right now!'

38. Corporal.

Original drawing by Richard Siegert.

I touched the handle of the Luger[39] resting in my trouser pocket. What a motherfucker! He'd probably spent the last four weeks sitting in the basement without sticking his nose outside, but had the audacity to remind me of my oath? I promised myself I'd kill him before anyone tried to put a rope around my neck. Later, I'd meet the *Wachtmeister* again in a situation that I could only have dreamed of.

39. P. 08 Luger-Parabellum 9mm semi-automatic pistol.

Chapter 12

Joseph Stalin and His Twin

The Zeppelin Meadow would get very lively during the day. One morning, the Russians tried to transport a heavy mortar[40] through it using three tractors, intending to fire at the Citadel. The mortar and tractors were destroyed with six of my missiles. No unnecessary shots for fear of exposing our position. Had the Russians noticed anything? I knew they'd probably start hunting us soon. It was the right time.

Two Russian IS-2 tanks came out of hiding and glided through the meadow. The huge Joseph Stalin tank with a 122mm calibre gun was the latest model among Russian heavy tanks. It was very difficult to destroy head on due to its heavy armour, but easy enough to damage from the side, where the fuel tanks were located. The sides of both tanks were facing me so surely my gun would obliterate them. I set the instruments to a distance of 1,200m. The first shot ready and I could get on with the second one. At the same time the missile hit, the giant exploded. The front tank's crew probably hadn't noticed anything yet, and the tank continued to glide forward as my second shot blew it up! The force of the explosion pushed the tank halfway into the ground. Now only two black clouds testified to the Russians' attempt to break through.

Nevertheless, the situation was becoming more and more dangerous for us. This was evidenced by the fact that the Russians hit the chimney of our house with an anti-tank gun, just as we are brewing our coffee. Then the driver of one of our assault guns was

40. Author error. It was an L/25 wz. 1931 203mm calibre howitzer.

Above and below: Two frames from a Russian film showing the use of the L/25 wz. 1931 during the fight for Poznań. (*Soviet newsreel*)

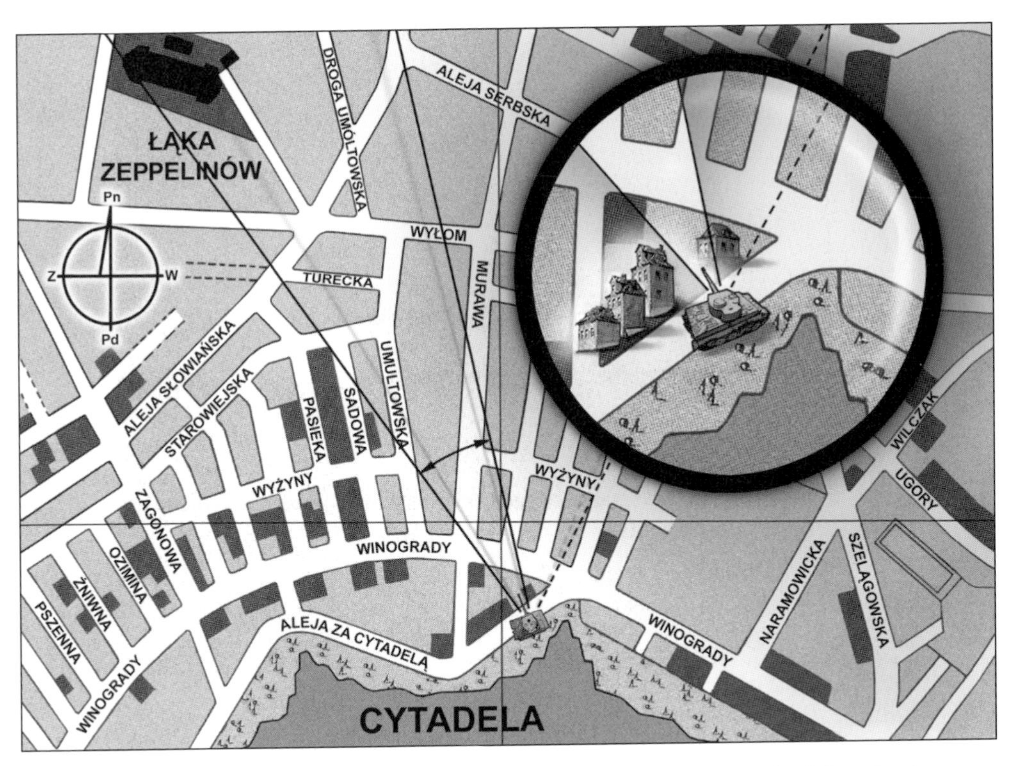

The northern area around the Citadel with the Tiger's position marked showing its field of fire towards the Zeppelin Meadow.

shot in the stomach while standing in the front door. Boarding the Tiger in daytime became increasingly risky and we planned to move the tank to a completely new location. 'Ivan' had already managed to take the nearby houses, and it was only a matter of time for snipers to establish themselves. We only left the tank at night to go and sleep in the basement, then boarded it again at dawn to continue our lookout. We hadn't showered or shaved for three weeks as there was no water. This was also a problem at the Citadel, where the water supply was failing, and the commandant had ordered that showering and shaving were strictly prohibited.

Chapter 13

Kurt Algner is Injured

There was a pump in the garden of the house we were living in which supplied us with water, but at what cost. It was under constant enemy fire as the sound of the arm being pumped up and down and the splash of the falling water created such a noise that the Russians opened fire with whatever they had. We usually took it in turns to go to the well. One evening, it was Kurt Algner's turn so he took two buckets and peeked out from the basement exit. 'Ivan' was pretty quiet, just the occasional shell passing through the air from time to time. We could hear the Soviet loudspeakers roaring: 'Comrades, do you want to go back to your homeland? Do you want to see your family and children again? Join us! Further fighting is futile! Tomorrow morning, at 7 o'clock Moscow time, you'll get the same wake-up call as today!" They were talking about 'Stalin's Organs' and the heaviest calibre guns whose shells fell on the Citadel and its surroundings. Kurt waited patiently before slowly sneaking across the garden to the pump, his feet wrapped in jumpers. When he got there, he crawled into a dugout (created for this very purpose) and we soon heard him starting to pump the water. It was quiet at first, but suddenly, what was that? Plop, Plop, Plop, Plop! Mortars! We were already in range! We hid in the basement as a salvo landed on top of us. Roof tiles and bricks fell right in front of us. Algner was still in the garden. I crawled out to him and could see a wound on his head bleeding profusely. I tore open my two dressings and tried to bandage him up before pulling him towards the basement. He had a huge hole in his thigh, so we bound his leg and tended the wound. Two infantry soldiers from our basement wanted to carry him to the Citadel, but the road there was under constant Russian crossfire. Running from crater to crater, constantly looking for cover, they managed to transport their injured comrade. An hour later, they reached the safe haven of the Citadel's casemates. We'd lost one of our most trusted companions and a noble soldier. Heckmann and I sat together all night, unable to sleep a wink.

Chapter 14

Do Unto Others as You Would Have Them Do to You

Leutnant Pehlen, an experienced infantry officer, arrived at dawn with the intention of taking down the Soviet sniper who'd been terrorising our neighbourhood. Armed with a rifle and scope, he took up position in the attic, removing a few of the roof tiles in order to improve his visibility. We barely spoke to each other. What was there to say? The situation was hopeless and we were merely fighting just to survive. I sat next to Pehle and watched both the Zeppelin Meadow and whatever was happening on the Russian side. As dawn broke they launched a rain of fire. Anti-tank shells exploded near the North Gate, with the slightest movement resulting in missiles flying over and covering everything in a shower of debris. Suddenly, Pehle picked up his rifle and I watched as he put the barrel through the roof opening and waited. I tried to hold my breath, but it was impossible: the incessant shaking caused my hands to tremble. At that moment, I saw his finger flex as the recoil forced the rifle butt back into his shoulder. Without a word, he handed me his binoculars and pointed the mansion on our left. I scanned the area and suddenly spotted a dead Russian hanging from a small staircase window, his rifle still in his hand.

After further shelling on the North Gate we could finally see the Russian anti-tank gun. It was located behind the corner of a house by Zeppelin Meadow, with just the barrel pointing out from behind a wall. Pehle outlined a plan: he'd destroy it at night with an assault group.

Two adjacent houses at Aleja Za Cytadelą (Steuben Allee). From the attic of the first house, *Leutnant* Pehle shot and killed a Russian sniper who'd positioned himself in the window of a neighbouring house. (*Soviet newsreel*)

The Tiger didn't have a sufficient field of fire as it was obstructed by the house.

It was a dark night. Infantry soldiers had watched the Russian positions during the day, taking note of all the smallest details such as the times of shift changes and where every lookout post was. The German assault group used the change of shift to their advantage and jumped over the trenches. The group consisted of three officers (cadets from the Infantry School who had been promoted during fighting in the fortress) equipped with Panzerfausts, and one *Obergefreiter* armed with a machine gun. Once behind the Russian lines, all four stood up and walked straight through the Zeppelin Meadow, occasionally stopping to listen to what was going on around them. They dropped to the ground when they heard footsteps getting closer, as the Russian shift change passed by the *Landsers* barely a metre away from them. The Russian soldier at the back knew that something was amiss. The German soldiers followed the Russians at a safe distance towards the house with the anti-tank gun hidden behind it. They suddenly heard the Russians being asked: 'Patrol?' They responded and then carried on. On the commander's order, the assault unit ducked and slowly crawled forwards, stopping just 60 metres from the house. They could clearly see the burning embers of the cigarettes the Russians were smoking, and could even hear their conversations as they hid on the ground behind a dirt track. The officers prepared their Panzerfausts as the commander took a few more deep breaths before giving the signal to fire. The shots hit the mansion, which burst into flames. A massive firework exploded. Our soldiers ran back breathlessly through the meadow, but not a single shot was fired at them. The *Obergefreiter* leapt into a Russian trench, shooting blindly left and right. The three officers ran past him and rushed towards our position. The Russians were so paralysed by this surprise attack that they didn't know what to do. Not a single shot was fired for nearly 20 minutes and there was a deathly silence. After a while, a signal shell was launched, and then another one, and a few more, but the spell was over. The next day, we assessed the damage through the binoculars: the house was in ruins, with the Russian anti-tank gun underneath it.

***

Only Fred Heckmann and I now remained from the 'old' Tiger crew. *Obergefreiter* Everoth, who seemed calm and deliberate, became our new loader. We sat in the tank day and night, waiting for the Russians to attack. One morning, while looking through my scope, I carefully rotated the turret and observed the terrain, which was covered in a light morning mist. It was only 4 o'clock in the morning so it was still quiet and there were a few hours left before the Russians gave us our usual wake-up call. At one point I saw someone setting up a Flak 8.8 out in the open. They must have lost any remaining decency, I thought to myself. Either they couldn't see anything or they'd gone completely mad. They were standing there as if they were on a parade! 'Fred, take the binoculars and look at those idiots ahead of us!' He stuck his head up through the turret hatch and held the binoculars to his eyes, before quickly drawing back and closing the hatch.

'It's a Pak 9.2! Distance 400, high-explosive, fire!' I'd had the gun in my sights for a while, so I pulled the trigger immediately. The shell howled out of the barrel and ... missed! I was preparing another shot when I suddenly heard shouting in my headphones: 'the gun's not retracting! I can't load the shell!' I inspected the damage: the gun had only pulled back two-thirds of the way and the missile was only half outside the barrel. This meant it couldn't be reloaded and prevented the lock from fully closing. Damn it!

Then, I heard Heckmann's voice again: 'Hurry! "Ivan" is turning his turret towards us!'

That's when I spotted the problem. The empty ammunition belt from our MG was laying on top of the cannon and jamming it. It must've fallen off during the recoil. I pulled out my knife and got to work. Heckmann then took over from me as I observed the situation through the scope. I turned my turret millimetre by millimetre, just as the Russians did with their gun. I also realised why I had missed earlier: the scope was set for an anti-tank shell, but the fragmenting shell was lighter and was directed by turning the turret to the right, which was then evened out through adequate adjustment to the scope. As I set it, I heard the crash of the cannon at the same time as I pulled the trigger. The shell left the barrel and hit the target. Two fragmenting and one anti-tank shell did the trick. The barrel of the 92 mm anti-tank gun lay twisted on the ground. 'Ivan' must've noticed us at last. Or had he?

I found the answer to that question the very next morning. It was six o'clock. Suddenly, a fire storm broke out, but it wasn't the usual Russian 'wake-up call'. Heavy artillery and 'Stalin's Organs' furiously pounded our forest: branches flew into the air, trees fell down, and the Tiger trembled with every blow. I hung on to the commander's hatch and pulled it down from the inside with all my might. Ever since it'd been hit by the Panzerfaust, it wouldn't close completely and instead just lay rather loosely on top. With each impact I was launched around 10 centimetres upwards. Every minute seemed like eternity. Would this hell ever end? My only thought was: 'Don't get a direct hit!' This hiss of bullets and explosions made a terrible noise, and I didn't know if it was the air pressure or the fear that made me shake so much.

The hell continued for another hour as wave after wave fell on us. Then, silence. I heard Heckmann's hoarse voice: 'Watch out, something's sure to start any minute'. I jumped up to look through the scope. I turned the turret slowly, but everything seemed to be in order. We had eluded death once again. 'Ivan' had quietened down. Did he think we were dead?

Then, on the edge of the meadow, next to the nearest house, a fence collapsed and the T-34 crawled out. After a while another appeared, then a third, and then a fourth. Four tanks, one after another, were coming at us from an acute angle. Keep calm! I started shooting using my tried and trusted method: aim for the last one first. From a distance of 1,200 metres, the missile struck and tore off the enemy tank's caterpillar. The T-34 span on its axis and stopped with its side facing towards me. It couldn't have been better. Another shot at its bathtub and the first of the tanks was on fire! The Russians jumped out of the burning wreckage. I heard Heckmann's voice: 'Distance 1,000 metres!' I calibrated my scope, aimed and fired. I hit the turret dead on. As the hatches opened up, smoke billowed out and the soldiers tried to escape.

Now I had to deal with the third one from the back. The distance was 800 metres at the most and everything happened just like it would on the training ground. The boom of the shot! Did I miss? Another! Finally! The tank was on fire and the hatches opened. However, the tank in front was still heading steadily in our direction. It suddenly started to increase its speed – it looked like it was trying to run away! The distance was 600 metres at best and it was now in the perfect position for me to hit it. My missile smashed into the left drive wheel and the T-34 turned 90°, buried in the ground. My second shot hit the side and soon after a huge explosion shook the air: an inner blast

Original drawing by Richard Siegert.

had torn it to pieces. I was no longer concerned about firing at the surviving Russians and only cared about saving my life and those of the other *Landsers*. The Russians who did manage to survive were no longer a threat to us.

The situation seemed to be getting even more hopeless: the Citadel was now under constant Soviet fire. The heaviest calibre mortars kept ploughing the area and the Russians shelled the Citadel all day long with a captured 210mm calibre railway gun.[41] Around 2,500 people had already died, and now the enemy began to attack from the north.

41. It was more likely a 280mm K5 railway gun as more of them were in use.

Chapter 15

The End is Nigh

On the afternoon of 22 February 1945, Major General Gonell and eight other battle group commanders had a final strategy meeting in his command bunker. He addressed them as follows: 'We are finished. I relieve you from following the Führer's order, commanding that no one alive can fall into the hands of the Russians. From midnight tonight, it's every man for himself!' On the same day, the last radiogram from Poznań was broadcast:

'At one o'clock in the morning, the final attack and attempt to break through the Zeppelin Meadow will take place.'

In the meantime, we were preparing ourselves for this endeavour. A rumour was spreading among the soldiers: 'The paratroopers will get us out of here! The Zeppelin Meadow must be recaptured before they land! The attack starts at one o'clock!'

I wasn't exactly thrilled by the thought of running across a kilometre-long open area straight into Russian fire. I wanted my life to be as expensive as possible. I discussed the situation with two infantry *Leutnants* and we decided to try to escape on our own, taking only our personal weapons with us. I took the submachine gun and put six spare magazines in my belt, as well as grenades and a Luger in my trouser pockets. We marched at midnight.

***

It was pitch black, and the light rain made our uniforms wet. The two officers knew every detail of the Russian trenches by heart thanks to their previous reconnaissance and combat missions. They took the lead, then Heckmann, with me acting as the rear defence. We crawled silently along 1,500 metres of empty road to the Russian fortifications. We were going to use the attack scheduled for one o'clock to our own advantage. Lying flat on the ground, we approached the Russians centimetre by centimetre. I was soaking wet and cold, but we were in front of the Russian lines. All of a sudden, a machine gun opened fire. What a crazy idea! We could easily distinguish the shots from the Spandaus[42] and the slower Soviet guns, which were now mowing down our soldiers as they charged the Russian positions shouting 'hurrah!' There was some sort of commotion among Russians ahead of us, as whole groups of them started running along the trenches to the left. This was our chance. We jumped out and ran in the same direction through the Russian trenches. Behind us, we heard Russian commanders shouting orders at their own men. The German 'hurrahs!' are now long gone, replaced with Russian 'urraahs!'

We crept towards the banks of the Warta before resting a while to catch our breath and regroup. I was freezing in my soaked uniform. In the distance, we could hear the sounds of fighting near the Citadel. There was a lively commotion in the cemetery we were about to pass through. Then, we heard a Russian shouting directly at us. We threw ourselves on the ground and, without moving, lay as flat as possible. More Russian screams. Nobody moved. A moment later we heard a faint 'slap!' and the blast of a hand grenade. The *Leutnant* next to me growled: 'Retreat!' and millimetre after millimetre, we crawled back noiselessly. The Russians were also afraid to leave their posts. After moving for about 30 metres in this fashion, we rose up and, bent over, crept away, wanting to leave the fire zone as quickly as possible. Any further efforts to escape had no chance of succeeding in these conditions and so after conferring with each other, we decided to head back to our dry shelter to change our clothes. We finally managed to pass the Russian lines and reach an empty road. We continued to crawl

42. A generic name for the MG 34 and MG 42.

back and, in the faint dawn light, around four o'clock in the morning, we reached our old basement quarters wet, dirty and exhausted. We took off our wet clothes, but unfortunately lacked any dry ones of our own to change into, and so could only use the uniforms left behind by German soldiers. I put on a camouflage jacket with no hood, but I didn't have any underwear. Less than two months later, these are the clothes I would be wearing when I was transported to exile in Karelia.

But what was happening at the Citadel in the meantime? The attempt to break out through the Zeppelin Meadow had been a complete disaster, and I pitied those who'd died following such a stupid order. Due to the hopelessness of the situation, Dr Geuder[43] had been ordered to offer the surrender of Festung Poznań to the Russians. Carrying a white flag, he headed out as an envoy to their positions. When he arrived, they took the flag and beat him severely with it,[44] before storming the Citadel. No more shots were fired and the crew was marched into captivity. The corridors full of wounded men were cleared out with flamethrowers.

---

43. During the fight for Poznań, Oberstabsarzt Dr Geuder was acting medical chief of staff chief for the stronghold.
44. In Dr Geuder's post-war written account there is no mention of the Russians beating him while he was acting as an envoy. It only contains information that he was brought to General Chuikov's main command post, located at the Poznań Opera. At the time of Major General Gonell's suicide, Dr Geuder was no longer at the Citadel. When writing about the doctor's beating, Richard Siegert was probably misguided by the information from G. Karwein's article entitled 'Der Grosse Treck' and published in *Neue Illustrierte* in 1958.

Chapter 16

Captured

According to certain reports from *Landsers*, the Russians simply blew up some of the underground corridors where the wounded were, but around 2,000 of them surrendered to the Russians in the Citadel. From our basement window we could see the Russian flow of traffic right up to the North Gate. They stormed the Citadel in groups, while vehicles full of loot left the place that had cost the blood of so many. I watched the area through binoculars and saw masses of people gathered in the Zeppelin Meadow. But what for? They were civilians and the majority of them women: I could easily recognise them by their headscarves. They also all had luggage.

The owner of the house we were living in, a 65-year-old Polish woman, was with us in the basement, along with her son, who was a stonemason. He'd been in Russian captivity once before and warned us that they'd not only take all of our valuables, but would also torture those with military titles and decorations. In light of this, we burned our medals and IDs and the officers ripped off their shoulder insignias – an act, it would later transpire, which would save some of their lives. We gave our valuables to Poles. They'd lost everything as a result of this miserable war, and such things no longer mattered to us. The woman's son brought us a white bedsheet so that we could make a white flag, which we then hung from the basement window. Wrapped in a blanket, I sat there and waited for what would happen next.

It was only an hour later that we heard the approaching Russians. The Polish woman was too afraid to go out and talk to them. Suddenly,

Clouds of smoke appear from the Citadel's casemates - probably due to the earlier use of flamethrowers inside, 23 February 1945. (*Wielkopolska Museum of the Fight for Independence*)

the doors bust wide open and 'Ivan' was standing there with a submachine gun pointed right at us. He shouted: '*War kaputt! Davai*!' [The war is finished! Come on!] He pointed towards the stairs leading to the outside. I was about to leave the basement first, but was then kicked back down. Someone grabbed me by the wrists and screamed: '*Urri? Urri?*' I didn't have a watch so instead they punched me in the jaw, resulting in blood pouring from my nose. Thousands of other German soldiers received the same treatment.

Our group was pushed out into the Zeppelin Meadow. We walked past dead soldiers and wrecks of burned out tank, which, half-sunk into the ground, resembled a cemetery. In front of us, one wounded soldier who was unable to walk was shot dead. '*Davai!*' They split us into groups and put us in the ruins of some house, where we were able

Russians posing for a photograph in front of one of the Citadel's fortifications that had been captured just a few hours earlier, 23 February 1945. (*Wielkopolska Museum of the Fight for Independence*)

to rest. One of the Russians came over and looked at our 'saperki'.[45] Those with shorter boots were better off and our footwear was taken away. If you were lucky you were given a pair of Russian boots, but the majority of prisoners had to go barefoot.

In the meantime, the Russians keep searching us, looking for something valuable they could take away. But we had nothing left. Even toothbrushes had been classified as 'culture'. Threats that they would shoot anyone if they found something didn't frighten us anymore, but we all knew that they wouldn't hesitate to do such thing. One of tankmen had a stuffed toy animal in his pocket, a gift from his wife. 'Ivan' took it away and threw it into a ditch. When the tankman

45. Tall military boots.

bent down to pick it up, 'Ivan' took out his 'Nagan'[46] (a Russian revolver firing 'dum-dum'[47] ammunition), and shot him in the head. I refused to believe that the gift was a lucky charm.

Major General Gonell took his own life. When his adjutant, Hauptmann von Kalm, had seen Dr Geuder being beaten from his command post, he shouted: 'The Russians are coming!' He then heard a shot from behind him. Gonell had committed suicide. His corpse was later displayed in front of the Opera with the following sign: 'This is the man responsible for Poznań's fate'. Out of thousands of German soldiers, only a few hundred, starved and exhausted, were taken prisoner.

46. Common name for the Soviet 7,62mm Nagant revolver.
47. Fragmentating bullets prohibited by the Geneva Convention. Usually a regular bullet with a cross-cut tip.

Chapter 17

Massacre and Death

In the meantime, more and more prisoners were gathering in the ruins of the house. New groups were being driven in from time to time. '*Davai*' is the first Russian word we learned. Hundreds of prisoners were sitting in the large meadow, wondering what the future would hold for them.

There was a civilian in a large group of Russian officers. He looked at the crowd and ordered: '*Ofizierrr! Davai!*' Any officers were picked out and lined up. There were seven of them, including an *Oberfeldwebel* who was unfortunate enough to have bought himself a brand new uniform from the uniform store. Nobody listened to him when he tried explaining that he wasn't an officer. They all had to leave their jackboots and were then thrown into a pigsty that was so small they couldn't even stand up straight. An 18-year-old Russian walked up and closed the gate before taking four steps backwards. He turned around, quickly grabbed his machine gun from his shoulder and emptied an entire magazine into the sty, a cigarette hanging from his lips as he did so. We gritted our teeth. The civilian chose a pair of boots and then left. We all started searching for medals. Anyone who had an Iron Cross First Class would be shot. A few of the SS soldiers had already been killed. The Russians were crazy with joy, riding through the crowd on small, coarse horses, shooting blindly all around them. I was afraid of being killed from such senseless shooting. The Russians buckled under the weight of their loot, which was generally made up of useless items, but they collected them with great pride. German cleaning rods in the form of chains were worn around the abdomen like watch chains. Their favourite souvenirs were

Polish militia.
(*Soviet newsreel*)

SA daggers. There was boundless joy after conquering the fascist stronghold that had managed to resist for five weeks. And as if that weren't enough, victory was achieved on 23 February, the Red Army's holiday day. The Russians couldn't have dreamed of a better date.

Prisoners kept multiplying and in the evening we were herded into barracks. There were around eighty of us and we could barely get in, but we were glad to have a roof over our heads. For the first time we met soldiers from the Polish Home Army.[48] They were a crazy group of young boys wearing civilian clothes with German belts and rifles on top. All of their equipment had been scavenged. It was impossible to sleep that night as the Poles kept appearing now and again looking for loot. They searched us, wanting to take our shoes and boots. I guess that's what they were missing. Officially, the Poles weren't allowed to do this and so tried to keep a low profile to avoid being seen by the Russians. We saw one 'Ivan' shoo one of them away with a kick. Apparently, the Russians had no intention of offering much to the Polish people.

48. They probably weren't members of the Home Army (who wouldn't likely show themselves openly to the Russians, bearing in mind what happened previously in Vilnius and Warsaw), but rather militiamen.

Chapter 18

The March of the 'Scourged' from Poznań

The next morning, we were lined up in a column and marched forward. '*Davai!*' Our group of beggars set off, not knowing where to. At first, the road ran through the city centre and, like the previous day, drunk Russians rode their horses through the column of prisoners, trampling and shooting at us blindly. We had to be careful. The streets were crawling with Russians and Polish: the civilians had left their hiding places and were crowding into the city to stare at their defeated oppressors. Both civilians and soldiers alike took out their anger on the prisoners and it didn't take long for us to find out that the middle of the column was the safest place to be. Those who walked on the edge risked receiving the most blows or being struck by rifle butts. Everyone tried to protect themselves as much as they could, and no one wanted to be pushed to the outside. We marched on incessantly. We had no idea how many prisoners there were, although we soon learned that some were being brought in from outside Poznań. We then noticed that we were marching down the same street we'd walked along two hours earlier, as I saw one of the Poles for the second time. He was standing in the doorway of a house shouting: 'Heil Hitler! Heil Hitler! Thanks be to our Führer!' while giving the 'German salute'. I witnessed similar scenes several more times.

At first, we didn't know what the Russians were planning to do with us, and we got the impression they didn't know themselves either as they kept marching us back and forth through the city. By the end of the day I think we'd walked about 20 km and were all very tired.

Column of German prisoners of war just after the surrender of Poznań. (*Soviet newsreel*)

We weren't given anything to eat or drink that evening, but we had no time to think about that. The third day was no different: from dawn to dusk we were marched through Poznań and the pitiful trudge of the prisoners increased even more. Sometimes, on an intersection, two marching columns would meet and the march would be halted in a race to make sure everyone was back in their position. Those who no longer had the strength were shot or bludgeoned to death with a rifle butt. It was a real-life Russian roulette and you had to be very careful not to get pushed to the outside of the column. During one of the stoppages, a Pole grabbed my clothes, turned me towards him and screamed: 'Well, were you so busy shooting you didn't have time to shower and shave?' before punching me in the nose. God, what must we all have looked like? I wasn't surprised, however, as we hadn't washed or shaved for nearly four weeks. We had beards like sailors. '*Davai! Davai!*' Our pathetic flock continued to walk ceaselessly around Poznań and when Russian tanks mercilessly drove right into the column, we barely had time to jump out of the way. Yet they continued to chase us! The prisoners in black, armoured uniforms were beaten and the only reason I managed to escape such a fate was I was wearing the camouflage jacket I'd put on after our reconnaissance mission. The population of Poznań flocked to the streets to participate in this terrible event. You could hear them screaming: 'You German pigs! This is what wanting the east gets you!' We had to atone for the numerous sins of others.

A rumour spread amongst us that in the evening we would be marched to the camp. Around four o'clock we were stood in front of the barracks surrounded with barbed wire. It was the so-called 'Dębiec Camp' (Dembsen). The gate, however, remained closed. After around two hours we heard someone shout: 'Back!' The camp was already full. As I'd been marching at the front of the column, close to the Russians escorting us, I wasn't beaten too badly. But now it was the opposite: I was at the back! I never want to experience those rifle butt blows ever again. I knew I had to try not to fall down, as those who did were doomed. We stopped in front of the barracks. The rooms were already occupied so we lay down outside and waited, wondering where we could possibly find shelter as it had started to rain. We greedily drank from the gutter to quench our thirst. It tasted horrible! Nobody dared to think about food. We were glad just to be alive and were too exhausted to feel hungry. We were finally let into the barracks and were pushed inside like sardines. Nobody said a

Prisoners. (*Soviet newsreel*)

word. At night we heard the roar of the cannons in the distance and the firing of anti-aircraft guns. It reminded us that, somewhere, the fight was still on-going. We'd completely forgotten about it already.

The fourth day of our captivity began in a similar way to the previous three. We were once again herded through Poznań: 'Onwards! *Davai*!' We were all exhausted and tried to support our weaker comrades as much as we could to stop them from falling down. Nobody could give up: it had to stop eventually.

***

We could hear the constant gunshots and Panzerfaust explosions. The Russians had discovered that the thousands of Panzerfausts they'd captured made wonderful props for photographs, and lined up with five or six Panzerfausts ready to fire. They fired on command and the Polish photographers had their hands full as the Russians wanted to capture the moment just as the fire came out from the front and rear of the barrel, right after taking a shot.

***

Soon after, they began herding us again: '*Davai!*' I reckon we walked about 15-20 km every day. We passed Russian field kitchens and my stomach painfully reminded me that there was such a thing as food. In the evening, we went back to the barracks surrounded with barbed wire. The gate opened and we were in the so-called 'police camp'.

Chapter 19

The 'Police Camp' & First '*Antifa*'

We were counted and then grouped seventy to a room. Unfortunately, 'Ivan' had clearly forgotten about giving us any food. I fell into a deep sleep, but when I woke up in the middle of the night I was soaked with sweat: was it really that hot or had I just had a nightmare? I had no idea. I could hardly move an inch. In the morning we heard the stomping of boots in the corridor: 'Get up! Line up in front of the barracks in your rooms!'

I was terribly thirsty and headed to the fire bucket with a borrowed dish to get some water. A Pole noticed what I was trying to do and came at me with a whip, but luckily I was much faster and managed to dodge out of the way, although I ended up losing my bowl.

After a while, the gate opened and we are once again moved out. Oh God, would this death march ever end?! We now noticed some Russian officers carrying cameras, who were filming our march of the conquered. It suddenly dawned on us that they wanted to prepare us for appearing on film. You could say that we'd become more photogenic during those few days: dirty, unshaven, beaten and starving, we certainly looked like beggars. 'This is how we wiped out the Fascists! Long live the heroic Red Army!' The men filming us buzzed around like crazy.

In the afternoon, we were guided back to the 'police camp'. My roommates, who were now all my close comrades, were all here. We were always determined not to be separated. At last, we heard: 'Two of you to get food!' There were sighs of relief all around. The Russians didn't want to abandon us all entirely to our fate! Two of our people returned with two buckets of tiny, boiled, unpeeled potatoes. We poured them out of the bucket in to the middle of the room and started counting. Everyone received two tiny potatoes: our first 'rations' for five days. I didn't see anyone peel their potatoes.

One evening, a foreign German soldier entered our room and said: 'Listen! I'm the cultural supervisor of your barracks. As you know, we've lost the war. It's not our fault, but it's our duty to ensure those responsible are brought to justice! Comrades, write your own reports entitled "I accuse!" and list all those louts who put guns in your hands and forced you to go! Name those bandits who forced you to prolong this war! You're under the protection of the heroic Red Army and the Red Cross, so you will be treated as prisoners of war according to the Geneva Convention!'

When I thought about the pigsty a few days before, I had my doubts. However, I believed that we would now be treated according to the directives of the Red Cross. The next morning, we all received a plate of 'thin' soup and a slice of bread each – our entire rations for the day.

We gradually got to know the camp as we explored the area in front of the barracks and tried to meet new friends. In one of the

Original drawing by Richard Siegert.

rooms I stumbled upon the *Unterofficier* who'd helped me put out the Tiger when it was on fire, and who'd carried an aerial bomb from the Redoubt Barracks. The Saxon lay on his back and whispered: 'There's no guard by the supplies'.

On my way back, I met an electrician in civilian clothes with a toolbox in his hands. Hey! I knew him! A familiar face that I'd definitely seen somewhere before! He looked at me in surprise, then turned around quickly and tried to disappear into one of the barracks. It was the head of the assault gun company who'd wanted to hang me. I was immediately reminded of the appeal the day before 'to name all of those bandits who forced you to prolong this war!', so I shouted:

'Hey, I guess we've met already!'

'I've never seen you before.'

What a pig!

'Get the fuck out man. Don't worry, I won't tell the Russians about you!'

He sped up and disappeared from my sight. He'd wanted to hang me and now he was working as an electrician for 'Ivan'!

A hairdresser came to our room next morning, and they didn't just shave our heads. At first, it was difficult to get used to being bald as it made us feel like criminals. We found it all very funny.

Our daily rations still consisted of a slice of bread and ladle of soup. Those who didn't have a dish didn't get any soup. We'd now started to feel our hunger, so we spent the days snooping around, trying to find something to eat. Near the kitchen barracks there were beets surrounded with barbed wire, but a fat Pole with a whip made sure nobody stole anything. Every day we had this image of the beets right in front of us. I tried to fish one out using some wire and pull it under the fence, but I was caught and locked overnight in a tower around 20 metres above ground. It was the famous 'police camp' fire tower, which had been used to dry fire hoses before war. It was missing a few planks in the floor, while the open windows made it really windy in there. I couldn't stand the cold, nor could my six other colleagues who were serving the same sentence for similar 'crimes'. They only let us out when the morning roll call started.

There was an assembly and roll call of prisoners every day, and if the numbers weren't right then it could go on for hours. Some individuals tried to escape, and perhaps a few of them even succeeded. But God help those who were caught and brought back. Such men would be beaten until blood was drawn, just to make an example of them.

Chapter 20

Guarded by a Polish Sentry

Note – *This chapter wasn't included in the German edition of* The Tiger from Poznań. *Just before its publication, the author decided to remove one of the paragraphs from the chapter 'Do Unto Others...', as he was concerned whether the events described would be seen as an attempt to justify the actions undertaken. However, as it concerns a story described in both additional chapters, he agreed to publish it in the Polish edition, with the following thoughts: 'When we destroyed a Russian anti-tank gun in the Zeppelin Meadow with our Tiger using two fragmenting shells and an armour-piercing one, we'd noticed a smoldering and smoking shape near the destroyed gun. I couldn't identify it through my periscope and so I turned to Fred and said: "Can you look through the binoculars and see what that is?" Then he screamed: "It's a Russian on fire. He's running away and might expose our position! Shoot him!" I responded: "Fred, I'm not shooting a wounded man because if I was in a similar situation I wouldn't like to be shot at." In the meantime, the Russian disappeared behind the corner of a house. The fact that the Pole didn't shoot me in the forest back then was, in my opinion, some sort of thank you for not shooting at that Russian. Both these events show that despite everything, people still show basic humanity even in war.'*

If you worked outside of the camp then it was possible to obtain some extra food. So when groups were organised for work at the airport, we volunteered. The work consisted of moving bombs and loading them on to Russian planes. We were forced to write 'Greetings Berlin' on them in chalk. The Russians were delighted to tell us that our German bombs were now falling on our wives and children. Fred's job was to scratch away the explosives from the fuses of the German bombs so that Russian fuses could be fitted. He turned yellow like a lemon from head to toe. I hope he wasn't contagious!

We were watched by a Polish militiaman while working at the airport. He was dressed in civilian clothes, with a white and red armband on his sleeve, wore Wehrmacht boots and carried a German rifle. We all thought he looked rather well-nourished after six years of war. The Russians told us that Polish sentries weren't allowed to take anything from us or bully us in any way. Back in the 'police camp', we witnessed one Pole searching our room for anything useful before some Russian kicked him out, literally. One day, the sentry saw us taking a break from carrying the bombs. After all, carrying 250 kg bombs in groups of four people using two poles wasn't easy. The sentry suddenly appeared from around the corner and saw us. '*Los! Los! Arbeit!*' [Go! Go! Work!], he shouted. Remembering the Russians' assurances, I told him to bring us some food first and then we'd be able to work. He told us he'd been in an SS camp where he'd worked for seventeen hours a day. 'You were in an SS camp?' I asked. 'It couldn't have been that bad since your neck is so fat it's wider than your head!'

He grabbed his rifle abruptly, reloaded and shouted: 'Get up!' He then started pushing the rifle barrel into my back and told me to march towards a grove. I thought to myself: 'What use are Russians' promises if a Pole tells them that he shot me as I tried to escape?' When we reached the grove he shouted: 'Halt!' I was sure this was the end for me, but no shots were fired and all I could hear was laughter.

When I cautiously turned around, I could see the rifle leaned up against a tree. The Pole reached into his pocket and took out a parcel wrapped in newspaper with two slices of bread inside. He handed one to me and a great weight lifted from my heart.

Chapter 21

On Our Way to Paradise

We were constantly drawing up escape plans, but the risks involved in such an undertaking were too great. I'm a rational person and so before I acted I wanted to make sure we had a carefully thought out plan.

We tried talking to a Pole at the airport who was refuelling and loading supplies into the planes. He also wanted to escape and asked if there was anyone amongst us who would know how to fly it. Fred Heckmann knew one: an officer who once worked as a test pilot at the Dornier factory. He knew several different types of aircraft, including foreign ones, so we added him to our commando group. He opted for an American twin-engine fast bomber with air-cooled radial engines that heated up quickly and allowed a speedy ascent.[49] We devised a plan to steal it and quickly fly over the bushes, but it all ended in fantasy. The next day we were unable to find the Pole and without him, getting close to any aircraft was impossible.

We spent our time as a working commando at the airport or dismantling Telefunken facilities. Using primitive methods, we loaded tons of lathes and other machines into freight trains leaving for Russia. Our rations hadn't changed for the better and so we gave up working at the airport. They'd only given us four potatoes a day, which wasn't fair considering the amount of work involved. We'd all lost a lot of weight and what's more, my leg wound had opened up again and had started festering. As a result, we mostly spent our days laying in the camp and waiting for what the next day would bring.

---

49. Most likely a Douglas B-20 Boston or North American B-25 Mitchell, which the USSR received under the terms of the Lend-Lease Act.

In the meantime, the number of POWs in the 'police camp' had increased even more. The Russians brought over men from the Piła stronghold, whose situation had been similar to ours here in Poznań. Those soldiers still had their personal belongings on them and were searched when they arrived. We estimated the pile of wedding rings confiscated from them was probably around 40 cm high. It was quite a loot already, but added to this were the personal fortunes of thousands of soldiers. The Russian propaganda machine started to gain momentum, describing how prisoners in Russia were given rations of nutritious soup served three times a day, porridge, and 600 grams of bread. It made us all hallucinate and delusional. While we were being split into working groups, it turned out that Group IV wouldn't go to Russia with the rest of us. Many of those poor, emaciated soldiers volunteered to go with us. What good was there waiting for them in Germany now the war was lost? Just more poverty. I didn't have to worry as I was put in the first group, even though I was so tired I could barely lay down on my bunk and nearly blacked out whenever I attempted to get up. I had to force myself to go for a wash or for a walk.

Thousands of German bombs captured by the Russians at Ławica airport. (*Soviet newsreel*)

We finally left in the middle of April. I was in the first transport from the 'police camp' heading for Russia. There were forty people in each carriage, with a small stove in the centre and bunks on the left and right for ten people on the top and bottom. Through the tiny windows of this cattle wagon, located just under the roof, we were able to see what was happening on the outside, although it was strictly forbidden to look.

The first station we recognised was Brest-Litovsk, where our train most likely stopped to refill the locomotive's water tank. It was also a chance to count the prisoners, which was done by a Russian *Leutnant* in a very dramatic way, hitting the carriage with a wooden hammer to see if we had broken the boards anywhere. Why not use the hammer to count us as well? Inside the carriage, we all had to crawl to one side as 'Ivan' sat in the middle and shouted: '*Davai*!' Everyone had to run past him in order to be counted. Those who weren't able to bend down quickly or jump aside were hit in the head with the hammer. The only way of getting past 'Ivan' was speed and so when the order was given, we ran past him as fast as we could so he wouldn't have time to hit us. Of course, someone got hit from time to time, getting a complementary anaesthesia for their efforts. If the situation hadn't been so serious, we would've had something to laugh at, but in these circumstances, however, forty men had to get to the other side of the carriage as quickly as they could. Injuries were inevitable. One of my friends broke his arm, which we could only bind up temporarily. Fred Heckmann said to me: 'Man, this moron with a hammer should've been put out of his misery earlier!' It's no wonder we often thought this way. As prisoners, we were treated like animals and our fate depended on our captors' moods. We were about to get fucked!

***

During our transportation we received slightly better food: 500 grams of bread and vegetable soup every day. The soup was not only filling, but also quite fatty and unfortunately, our bodies had forgotten what to do with such food and so I suffered from terrible diarrhoea. My hunger soon disappeared and I had to force myself to eat. This carried on for fourteen days. We had no idea where we were going: the guards didn't talk to us and the civilians we saw at the railway stations weren't allowed to approach us. We couldn't find out any information. During each stop, two people were allowed to approach the locomotive to bring coal for the fire. Based on the sun's position, we guessed we were heading east and I realised we were approaching Vitebsk. I knew that place by heart: a bridge over a river and a city floating behind it. We turned on an arc and were now heading continuously north, travelling day and night without stopping. Nothing happened besides prisoner counts and meals as we all fell into apathy. We'd endured the first stage of our captivity and hoped that this wasn't what it'd be like for the rest of our lives. We waited patiently and finally reached our destination after two weeks. It'd been snowing for days and when we looked outside, everywhere was completely white.

We suddenly heard: 'Prepare to leave the train!' We were about 400 km north of Leningrad. When the doors opened, all you could see as far as the horizon was white. On our left were the roofs of three houses, which was supposedly our camp. We were ordered to dismantle the carriage roofs and build our bunks from them. The houses themselves were empty, with no windows or doors. Everyone took a plank from the carriage, put their dishes under their arms, and climbed off. I was so weak I could barely stand on my own. The brightness of all the white stung my eyes after having spent what felt like an eternity in a pitch-black carriage. The beggar's parade started marching again, each of us carrying a wooden plank on their back as we climbed the hill. I felt like Jesus carrying his own cross and knew I certainly wasn't looking my best. I heard one of the *Landsers* behind me say: 'This young one won't last long'. This was my reward for my honesty. After all, I wouldn't have been in this position if I'd left Poznań at the right moment. I'd had several chances, but never took the opportunity. Now, with an actual cross on my back, I kept climbing to the top. My torment would continue for the next four and a half years.

During following days we were busy helping with the construction of the bunks and preparing the interiors of the houses. Despite being weak, I managed to wash myself and move around a little every day. However, many of the men simply lay down on their bunks apathetically before dying from exhaustion. Our transport, which had originally amounted to 2,000 people, was in a sorry state. Many of us had diarrhoea and couldn't fully recover. Around thirty-five people died every day, but we couldn't bury the corpses because the ground was frozen and so we just piled them behind the barracks. I managed to obtain a jacket from a fallen comrade, meaning I finally had something warm to wear. Its former owner certainly didn't need it anymore.

We lived in the main camp for four weeks before being split into groups and transferred to the outer camps. Those four weeks were supposed to be a form of quarantine and recreational time for us. I was sent to the 'brick factory camp', while Fred Heckmann (my driver) and Fred Leupold (my *Gefreiter* friend from Poznań) were held in the main camp by the Russians. Of the 'original' Tiger crew, only Fred Heckmann and I were still alive.

Heckmann worked in a sawmill near Lake Onega. His commando consisted of seventy people, while his brigade was made up of four people. They pulled logs from the lake with a rope hoist and then put them in to piles. After dividing people into working groups, nobody cared about the brigade any more. Heckmann, who'd always loved danger, came up with an escape plan: he hated being held prisoner. Along with three comrades, for a week he saved up one slice of bread out of our daily rations and toasted it. This was supposed to serve as their food for the first few days of their journey.

One day, before sunrise, they attempted their escape. Lying flat on their stomachs on a log raft, they paddled close to the bank, avoiding the sentries, before marching south. As the road through the Karelian marches was quite busy, the only possible route for Heckmann and his comrades was along the railway tracks. However, they still needed to avoid all of the railway buildings. The water had reached up to their waists and their long coats were soaked. Having been walking for two days, and still exhausted and starving from their captivity, they were now even more hungry and cold. To make walking easier they'd cut their coats short, but unfortunately, misfortune was right around the corner.

Walking along the railway tracks they stumbled upon some railway workers. The fugitives ran and hid in the swamps, but not for long. Guards were sweeping the area and their dogs, who were specially trained to hunt for prisoners, were barking furiously. Heckmann and his colleague, a former paratrooper, were shot by a machine gun and he was hit in the chest by fourteen bullets. He died in the swamp and that is how I became the only surviving crew member of the Tiger from Poznań.

Original drawing by Richard Siegert.

Part II

Captivity

The ‘Brick Factory Camp’ in Sulasch-Gora, near Petrozavodsk

Chapter 22

The 'Brick Factory Camp'

After a four-week quarantine in the main camp in Petrozavodsk, the capital of the lands captured from Finland, we were transferred to other camps, thus freeing up space for new prisoners.

However, our health didn't improve during those four weeks. We all felt equally bad, despite receiving daily food rations consisting of 600 grams of bread and soup served three times a day. I suspect it was caused by our previous stay in the 'police camp' in Poznań, where we almost starved to death. Half of us had dysentery, while the rest suffered from chronic diarrhoea at best. No one received any proper medicine and we'd all come to terms with our fate. We'd already stopped mentioning our illnesses to our camp doctor, Dr Mannel from Heidelberg, who at one point conducted bowel surgery with a razor, but without any anaesthetic. I was angry that my body wouldn't accept such fairly decent food, not to mention the pain in my anus caused by constant excretion. I could barely get through the morning assembly, which often took several hours, and during which I would lay down on the ground and get up only when it was my turn. Getting up and washing myself in the ice-cold water from a stream that ran through the camp was a huge success for me. Some of us didn't even have the strength to do that and just died of exhaustion.

One day, my name was called out and I found myself in a group assigned to different camp. When the time came to leave, I couldn't see a single familiar face all around me. Old friends, who until now had tried to stick together, had been separated. A new, unknown future awaited us. Our column marched a short distance beside the houses before moving through a more uninhabited landscape. We changed direction when we came to an intersection, the Russians intending to confuse us by taking us on a detour, and so our pathetic group kept marching on. In Karelia, the onset of June meant the snow began to melt. Banks of snow several metres high flanked both sides of the road, while bushes and trees bent under its weight. The melt water ran along the ditches. We'd ben marching for several hours and were so thirsty, but I had to force myself not to think about the melt water that was so close at hand. The sun burned my shaved head and my lips were dry as parchment. All I could think about was my thirst and the water next to me. As I marched, I kept looking down at it and the grass growing in it. Everything else ceased to exist. I finally threw my miserable and dehydrated body into the ice-cold water and gulped greedily to quench my thirst. 'I already had dysentery,' I thought to myself, 'what else could go wrong?' Just then, someone grabbed me sharply by my collar and pulled me out, but at least the thirst was gone.

On that day we marched about 15 kilometres, finally arriving, nearly dead with exhaustion, at the destination that was to be our camp for next few years. On the edge of a pine forest, to the left of the road, we could see two large two-story wooden houses. The rooms were empty and the windows were missing. There were huge water tanks on the roofs for fighting fires, with two sloping ladders leading up to them. I'd never seen anything like it before. Later, I found out that the houses had formerly been police barracks, but the Finns had given them over to the Russians during the war. Each room housed twenty people, and we all fell down exhausted right where we stood. The following morning we found that bedbugs had bitten our necks and wrists. Something else happened as well: I didn't have to go to the toilet. And so it remained. The icy water had apparently cured my diarrhoea. There was no other explanation.

During the next few days, our time was driving posts into the ground, stretching barbed wire and building four watchtowers at the corners of the fenced area. We built our prison with our own bare hands. Thankfully, we had no idea what else awaited us. We were glad to have survived the first few days: no one could've imagined something worse was to come.

Besides the two houses outside it, there was nothing else but trees all around the camp. Our guards moved into the houses, although the guards who'd brought us there were soon replaced by uniformed women with shaved heads: Russian prisoners. Their names were tattooed on their left arms: Dusia, Nadya, Tamara. It was the easiest way of identifying them. They were our new guards who were supposed to keep an eye on us as we worked. They would keep their

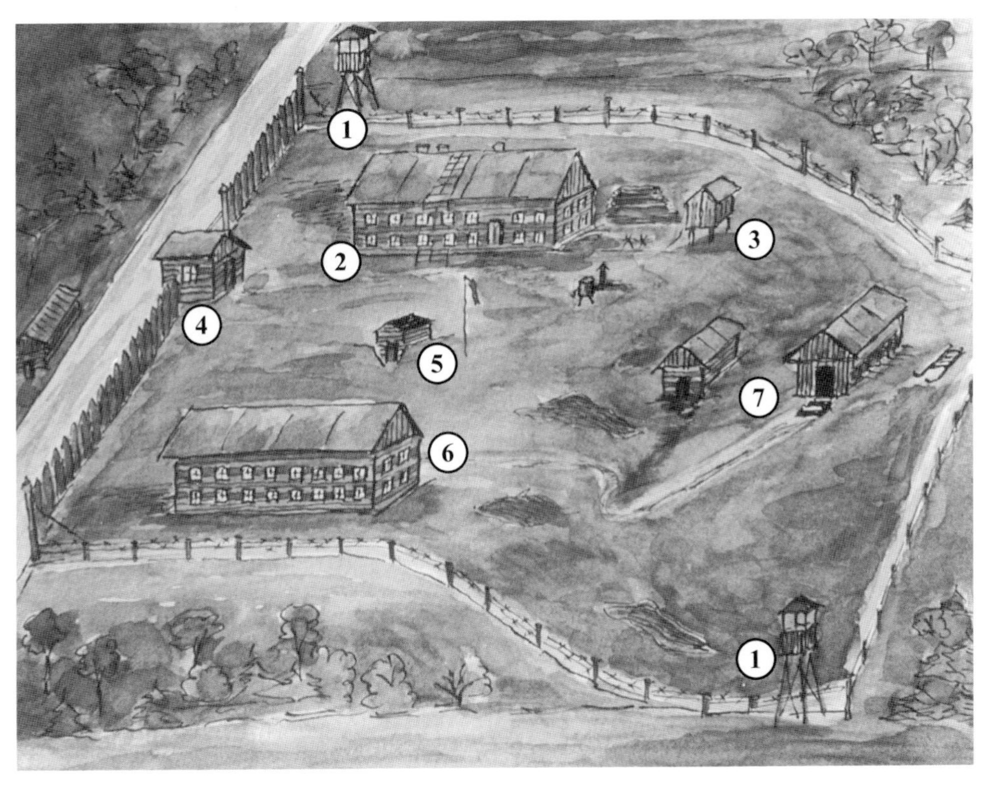

Richard Siegert's painting of the prisoner of war camp in Sulasch-Gora, in Karelia.

1. Watch towers
2. Utility rooms & kitchen
3. Clothes storage
5. Karcer
6. Living quarters for prisoners (18 rooms, 20 people per room)
7. Latrines

fingers on the triggers of their guns, then report on our efforts in the evenings. They must've pitied us because they always said: '*Charaszo rabotajut!*'[50]

In the meantime, our bunkbeds were built and put in place, along with glass for the windows. It's ironic to say that we were to be housed as comfortably as possible. Soon after, the first prisoners were sent to work in a Finnish brick factory nearby. Using basic and worn-out tools, we had to clean the mortar from old bricks and put them into piles. A rumour soon spread that we were going to rebuild the factory, but we all refused to believe that we would have to fire bricks. How wrong we were.

A normal day in the camp looked like this: get up, eat one slice of stale bread and a weird-looking brown soup, then go to work. Around noon, it was the same food again and then work until nightfall. After this we would work inside the camp: chopping wood for our rooms and the kitchen, and other tasks. We slept on bare bunks, without even a bag of straw, and usually in wet clothes. We were constantly hurried to work with '*Bystra! Bystra!*'[51] It wasn't just the Russians who rushed us. There was a German amongst us who was appointed deputy to the Russian commandant, Captain Sutschkov, who'd previously run a Partisan school in Leningrad. The deputy was Heinrich Albers, from Emden, and he often behaved worse than any of the Russians, beating us with his baton. Every day he would search for a new victim, with any little misdemeanour being punished by twenty-five strikes to the bare backside with his truncheon. We later found out that he'd obtained his position after betraying his fellow naval officers. They'd all worked in a sawmill together, along with a Finnish prisoner, and had drawn up an escape plan, but Albers handed them over to the Russians. As the saying goes: 'A traitor is the biggest bastard in the whole country'. After two years, Albers disappeared from our camp.

---

50. They're working well.
51. 'Quickly! Quickly!'

The Russians were probably worried that we’d hurt him. A former Austrian forest ranger was then promoted to deputy, who usually took our side during clashes with the Russians and basically made our lives much more bearable.

As I’ve previously mentioned, after arriving in May 1945 we gradually got to know our new workplace: the old brick factory. The kiln consisted of a pile of frozen and icy bricks, with our first task being to clean the bricks of mortar and then stack them. We then built a new kiln with these bricks, the so-called ‘field kiln’, which would then be used to fire the bricks needed to build a new brick factory. The conditions were very primitive, which is why we all thought the whole undertaking impossible, but we were wrong.

All of the work was supervised by a Russian ‘*prorab*’ (a kind of foreman), who devised the following incentives for our work:

Those who achieved 100 per cent of the target would receive 600 grams of bread and three servings of first-rate soup, while those

Work commandos composed of German prisoners of war in one of the camps in northern Russia. (*Marcin Krzysztoń*)

who reached 80 per cent of the target received 400 grams of bread and a second-rate soup. However, the requirements were so high that most people only received around 200 grams of bread and fourth-rate soup. This was too little to live on, so hunger and a will to survive motivated us to work at top speed. We wanted to break this vicious circle and so we handed all management over to a German structural engineer. The first thing he did was to hire a Russian interpreter and get his hands on a Russian working standards book. As it turned out, the Russians had been lying to us: they'd only paid us for one job, for example, when we'd actually carried out three.

The result of our four years of work was a brick factory with an eighteen-chamber kiln, which was constantly kept lit. During one shift we fired 18,000 bricks, which, considering we worked three shifts a day every day, meant around 1.5 million bricks per month! The forest brigade shouldn't be forgotten either, as they had to supply all of the wood for the kiln. That's what hunger can help you to achieve.

Chapter 23

Water Supply

For the 380 people in the camp, the most important source of nutrition was the daily soup. In order to prepare it, water had to be brought from a well outside the camp. Such a task was especially dreaded during the winter, so it often served as a punishment for certain brigades. Our leader, a former *Feldwebel*, eagerly delegated people for the task in order to please the Russians. In the camp environment, just as before, there were those who might formally have been called the 'nation's pets' and had been like that from birth.

Winter in Karelia, with freezing winds from the sea and temperatures between –25°C and –35°C, often made the task of getting water particularly unbearable. The main form of transportation were Russian sleds, with three wooden barrels on top of them, and six people using a mass of ropes to pull it along like a dog sled team. After putting on furs and face coverings, we'd receive an order and start running towards the well. I felt like a dog every time. Next to the well was a log cabin where a civilian lived. They'd let three of us inside to warm up while the rest of the group filled the barrels with water. Then it was the others' turn to rest, but they had twice the job. Pulling the water out of the well was the most difficult part of the whole procedure. Our gloves would freeze to the pole so we'd have to take them off. Working in turns of three was almost unbearable and even though we worked as fast as we could, the water would spill out and freeze. Throughout the winter, a mountain of ice formed around a metre from the well. We'd put our vehicle on top of it and then roll it down again, taking care not to do this too quickly for fear of it tipping over, which would mean doing to whole thing all over again, before returning to camp as quickly as we could. Our fingers regularly froze and when the wind blew directly into our faces, the breath under our balaclavas turned to icicles. Nevertheless, it meant we'd be able to have another serving of soup.

Chapter 24

Christmas 1945

The temperature had been –30°C for a week. In the brick factory we continued to clean the bricks and stack them into piles. We'd made ourselves wooden clogs and even gloves from some remaining goats' fur (Russian spoils from Finland). We also used the fur to protect our noses by making coverings tied to our hats, but your arms and legs were the most vulnerable to the cold. Despite it being prohibited to do so, we'd try to get to the brick factory's drying room as often as we could as it was possible to get some warmth there. If we were caught, a Russian guard would hit us with his rifle butt, but if it was a Russian foreman, the so-called '*prorab*', then he'd usually just give us a warning.

One day, I found myself working outside with an orchestral violinist. He was too scared to go to the fire to warm up and was simply afraid of being beaten. On that particular day the temperature outside had dropped to –34°C. If only it'd dropped below –35°C, any outside work would have to have been halted. The north-easterly wind blew in from the sea all day and it was bitterly cold. In the evening, when we returned to the camp, my new companion took off his gloves and his hands were blue with cold. His fingers were frost-bitten and he'd never be able to play his violin again. I guess that's why he went crazy soon after: we'd often see him sitting on a pile of rubble, conducting. His hair turned grey overnight, too, and was suddenly completely white.

Finally, in the lead up to Christmas, we were allowed to have a fire in our rooms for an hour, but only for the lucky few who'd managed to sneak in dry pieces of wood under their coats. The guards would often take it away as they needed it for their own fires. After about an hour, a sentry came in and ordered us to put out the fire. Behind him was our instructor from the camp's 'anti-fascist group', who was supposed to re-educate us politically. He addressed us: 'Dear comrades, we thank the heroic Red Army for allowing us to celebrate Christmas Eve. Let us sing '*Silent Night, Holy Night'* together'. A few minutes earlier, a Russian guard had thrown the small Christmas tree we'd decorated with clay baubles out of the window.

Chapter 25

Antifa

The Russians set up an anti-fascist group in each camp, which was tasked with making us familiar with the communist ideology. Its members didn't have to work and even received additional food from the kitchen. We called them '*ladle-Antifa*'. Their leader and camp instructor was called Karl Seibt, who came from Worms, Germany. He'd explained to the Russians that as a former industrial business administrator, he'd been interned by the Nazis and locked up in a concentration camp, but claimed that he 'supported' the communist worker's union. His assistant was a man called Müller, who constantly wore a militia hat and tried to convince us that he, too, had been in the same concentration camp. However, we all thought he was just a common criminal rather than a political prisoner, and even suspected him of espionage. The third and only decent man in this group was Paul Haubold, a school headmaster from Nossen, near Dresden. Once, when the Russians refused to give me my post, supposedly as a punishment for not meeting my daily quota, he let me read it in my room and we became friends. As for the anti-fascist group, he told me plain and simple that everyone just wanted to get back home. He was only 44, so I understood him completely.

After two years, we were finally allowed to write letters home, but not by our own hand. Instead, we had to dictate the twenty-five words we were entitled to whilst standing in the anti-fascist group's office. Seibt, the instructor, asked me to write some additional greetings on my postcard as he noticed I was sending it to Hindelang, where some friends of his also lived. My parents were supposed to pass the postcards on, but thankfully my mother kept them. When I finally arrived back home, I found the cards containing the greetings for the Schiebel family from Hindelang. I later learned that the family were the owners of a basement bar in Hindelang and that the alleged business administrator was working there as a waiter.

Chapter 26

Spring at Last

We all suffered greatly from poor nutrition and vitamin deficiency such as scurvy during the first winter. There were ulcers on our skin that turned purple like boils and had to be cut open. Our health worried the camp doctor, but they could do nothing about it, saying only that we'd all be alright if we had some eggs, butter and pork. As for the vitamin C deficiency, he recommended we cut down branches from the nearby pine forest, chop them into chips and use them to brew an infusion. From then on, each of us had to drink a ladle of this beverage every morning.

Near the end of May, the snow finally began to melt. The trees dusted off the white fuzz, green leaves appeared under the snow on the birches, and the pines trees developed new shoots, up to 5cm long. The daily morning route to the brick factory led along the edge of the forest and one day someone discovered that you could eat the pine shoots by taking them out of their shells. We all knew this was much tastier than the brown drink brewed from boiled old pine needles. Within three days, the trees were plucked as if they'd been hit by a locust swarm. Not a single fresh shoot remained. Unfortunately, we soon found out that this hadn't been such a good idea, as the resin from the shoots stuck our intestines together. We gave up the pine needles!

***

The camp was plagued by bedbugs. The lights were on the whole night, but nevertheless, we still heard the characteristic sound of insects falling from the ceiling and bouncing off the tin cans we used for dishes. They were everywhere: in the walls and the gaps between the planks of our bunkbeds. We used to sleep in our clothes as we had no straw mattresses, and even slept in our boots as a result of the bedbugs, even though we were forbidden to do so. A Pole, who acted as an interpreter, checked our room every evening and shouted: 'Nobody sleeps in their shoes! It's uncultured!' We'd try to control the plague on our days off by dismantling our wooden bunks and throwing the individual planks briefly into the fire to burn the bedbugs. After this, we'd have peace for a short while.

One day, I noticed a red stain in the 'death zone', an area separated by barbed wire. It was a wild strawberry that had somehow managed to grow in such a place. I couldn't take my eyes off it or stop thinking about it. I had to have it! I asked my old friend Schimura for help as he also wasn't scared to go and get it, despite the fact it was growing in the 'death zone'. The place was only visible from the watchtower, where a young guard with a rifle was on duty. We had a good view of the tower from the upper window of our quarters, and while the rest of us were busy burning the bedbugs, I hid behind the barrack and stared at the window where my friend Schimura was watching the Russian guard. As the guard turned around, Schimura gave me a sign and I crawled under the barbed wire. I slid my hand under more barbed wire on the edge of the 'death zone' and grabbed the berry. With the prize in my hand, I headed back to safety. If the guard had turned just seconds earlier, I would've paid the ultimate price. I'd risked my life for one wild strawberry. What times we were living in.

Chapter 27

Work Commandos

In the middle of winter, we were asked who could ski. Nobody really knew what was going on, after all, it was usually between –25°C and –30°C in the Karelian tundra. However, some Austrians did come forward, including two from our room: Matthias Binder, from Salzburg, and Dauerböck, from Steiermark. They were given Finnish running skis, along with an axe and a saw, and sent out into the Karelian tundra. The Russian surveyor had used a compass and, according to his instructions, they were to dig a road into the forest. We learned later that the terrain was a swamp and was only accessible during the winter when it was frozen over. Using hollow roads, the plan was to measure the differences in altitude of the surrounding area and start draining the swamp.

Our commando worked hard throughout the winter, but sadly our efforts didn't come to a halt at the beginning of spring, or even the first thaw. We dreaded the upcoming days when we'd be chopping down trees and bushes, all the while stood knee-deep in water, which wasn't only inconvenient, but very unhealthy. The whole situation was very depressing. We'd expected better work, but just went from one gutter to the next.

Every 1 May we received new clothes for the year, and our winter outfits, consisting of insulated trousers and furs, were replaced with a summer jumpsuit. At that time of the year, Lake Onega was still under ice approximately 1 metre thick, meaning planes could land on it and trucks could drive across it. These were the conditions in which we worked in the swamp. In Karelia, winter came very suddenly, as did summer. Snow disappeared from the trees, which were already green beneath it, and new leaves grew on the birch trees. As the sun started to burn more mercilessly from one day to the next, a new plague revealed itself: mosquitoes. Several prisoners developed a fever almost instantly. The Russian doctor called it 'Volyn fever' [trench fever], but none of us understood what that meant. One day I was assigned to this work. It was a living hell. Every time I went to take a step, a swarm of mosquitoes appeared and attacked eyes, nose and ears. One time, when I angrily wove my axe around in frustration, I cut off my thumb nail in the process.

At this point, I must mention an invention our Russian engineer came up with; a kind of tin helmet with a built-in protective mosquito net. He'd made it from an aluminium bowl from his 'babushka' [grandmother] by punching holes around the outer edge and then gluing a piece of curtain on the inside. He'd wear it on his head and I must admit it worked quite well.

When working in the swamp, however, there was something else that grabbed my attention. I noticed quite a significant number of snakes and almost immediately remembered a story from my childhood. My uncle had learned to cook after working as a waiter in Paris and he told me about one of the dishes on the menu there: 'stuffed snakes'. In the past I'd always been afraid of snakes, but now I was more afraid of starving to death and so I started hunting right away.

First, I made myself a knife from a broken piece of a circular saw and then, armed with a stick I began to hunt. The snakes would usually run away immediately, but that's when I'd stun them with a blow to the back of their head and finish them off with my boot. I'd then take my knife and cut off their heads before removing their skin, cutting open their belly and ripping their guts out. Unfortunately, snakes aren't particularly meaty, but four of them would fill my bowl. Without any salt, spices, or French chef's recipes, the meat was pretty tasteless, but at least I had something in my stomach.

One day I hunted a long, black snake that was hiding from me in a burrow. I tried to scare him out with a stick, but then he suddenly jumped out of his hiding place nearly a metre high. I leaped back and hit it with my stick somewhere behind its neck and then held it down with my leg. I wanted to take it back to the camp alive and so I split the stick and put the snake between the two pieces. The camp commandant later told me that the snake was venomous and that I was lucky not to have been bitten.

Later, during summer, our measuring commando was 'rebranded' into a drilling commando. In some places we dug to a depth of 15 metres and extracted mineral samples. As a result, we learned that the soil there consisted of a 6-metre layer of peat, followed by an 8-metere layer of clay. After the ground had been drained, the plan was to build another brick factory there. Dried peat would be used as fuel and the huge amounts of clay would be used to produce the bricks. This wouldn't be our task, however, as a large group of Russian prisoners had been assigned to this job, and I pitied them when I thought about the swamp and the mosquitoes.

Chapter 28

Cadet Kischkl

Everyone knew Kischkl following the failed escape attempt he carried out with Alex Kuhl, a medic. They'd tried to cross the Karelian tundra in temperatures of –20 to –30°C, some 2,000 kilometres from the border of East Prussia, but were soon caught and then beaten. A Russian guard hit Alex Kuhl five times in the head with the handle of his 'Nagan' pistol, leaving five holes in his skull and causing him to lose his mind. Afterwards, he was transported to Leningrad, while Kischkl was left with a crushed collarbone.

We met while cutting wood for the new brick factory. Each of us had to split and place 18 m^3 of wood delivered from Finland. It had to be cut by the metre so as to later serve as firewood for the kiln. If we achieved 100 per cent of our target then we received 600 grams of bread and three servings of first-rate soup every day. But the conditions were very hard and we were so weak we could only manage to complete around 60 per cent of the target, meaning we received 400 grams of bread and a fourth-rate soup, which we called 'Ludwig'. What's more we were working outside in temperatures of -25°C, bending under the weight of the Finnish furs and wearing masks over our faces to protect us from the freezing cold. I soon developed tendonitis in my right arm and could barely hold an axe. The Russian doctor gave me a sling, but didn't stop me from working. The Russian labour officer stated that I could cut the wood with my left arm and assigned a second person to help me: the ex-cadet from Infantry Midshipmen School, Kischkl. He was also wearing a sling and in addition to the usual eight hours of work, he was also assigned other tasks such as cleaning the toilets, all as a punishment for trying to escape.

I worked day and night without any respite, but he wasn't interested in having his spirit broken and so his main objective was to get to the infirmary. He seemed to think I was the right man to help him achieve his goal and so decided that I'd be the one to help him. According to him it was all very easy, I simply had to break his arm. He said that all he had to do was put his hand on the edge of the table then I'd break the protruding part with just one blow. It was so easy, anyone could do it. I told him he was out of his mind and that I wasn't a doctor and could never do such as thing.

But he kept talking about it all the time we worked together. He dreamed of lying in the infirmary where he'd receive 500 grams of bread and a thick soup three times a day. Lying there in the warmth, without any work, leaving the frost outside. I used to feel a great relief when the day was finally over and his chattering ceased. Unfortunately, however, the next day he'd just start all over again. He tried to win me over by appealing to my sense of honour, calling me an irresponsible coward. According to him, with one blow I could change all that, but instead preferred to watch him suffer and die slowly.

I don't remember how long it took, but eventually he managed to persuade me to help him. If anything, I just agreed to it to shut him up. Kischkl told me what to do: he'd put his elbow on a pile of bricks and I was to hit it as hard as I could with a wooden club. I practised by hitting the bricks first with all my might and after complimenting me on my efforts, he told me to do it again, but this time hit his arm. I grabbed the club, all the while telling myself that I was only doing what he was telling me to do. He didn't even groan. His eyes merely rolled backwards and he dropped to the ground like a felled tree.

Our workplace was right by the kiln wall. There were stairs leading to a mezzanine where a fire was always kept burning and was therefore always warm. However, we weren't allowed to go there. With Kischl lying on the ground unconscious, the men went running to our group's supervisor Hauser. I told him that we needed to warm him up in the mezzanine and as we climbed the ladder, taking care not to be spotted by the Russian guard, Kischkl fell down headfirst. He was carried back to camp on a stretcher and then transported to a hospital in Petrozavodsk. I hoped he hadn't suffered any permanent damage and that the better treatment he'd receive would help compensate for the pain. After a few weeks he returned to the camp and told me that I hadn't actually broken his arm, but had managed to separate the muscle from the bone when I struck him. Like I said, I needed the practice.

At the time, I didn't really think these events would have any impact on my life, and it only really affected me after I'd recovered from the tendonitis and went back to my old woodcutting team. The unit's supervisor, Hauser, had heard that I'd once called him a 'mug' and wanted revenge. He assigned me to a job cutting metre-long pieces of wood. They'd been put to one side as they were particularly misshapen and therefore more difficult to work with. My efficiency dropped down to 40 per cent so I only received 200 grams of bread and fourth-rate soup. As the days went by and I felt my energy fading, I had no hope that the situation would improve. Suddenly, I felt rebellious: I, too, wasn't going to let them crush me. It was just how Kischkl had felt. In my mind I saw myself lying in the hospital, not working in -30°C cold, but instead receiving 500 grams of bread three times a day with each serving of thick soup. All I had to do was get there.

I decided to injure my foot and the idea haunted me so much that I soon accepted it. First, I needed to have some practice in order to do it correctly. I carved an incision into a trunk with an axe and used it to practise. I needed to have a 'steady hand' so as not to injure myself permanently. After having survived my first winter in Russia, I already knew the difficulties soldiers had who'd suffered

Painting by Richard Siegert showing prisoners felling trees at the camp in Sulasch-Gora, Karelia.

frostbite on their big toes, so I decided to hit my second toe to avoid difficulty walking. I practised hitting the mark in the trunk all day long. The thought of the hospital soon became an obsession, but I couldn't take that final step. At the end of the day, I told myself I'd do it tomorrow.

When I was standing in front of my pile of wood again the next day, clad in thick fur, with a temperature of –25°C, I knew for certain that that day I wouldn't be returning to the camp with the others. But first I had to check my accuracy, so I made another mark in the trunk and practised some more. In the meantime, I also made sure I did my job as I didn't want anyone to find my behaviour suspicious. The temperature kept dropping, my hands were freezing and my aim was getting worse and worse. Eventually, the day was over and after eight hours of work, I'd chickened out once again.

On my way back to the camp I cried with anger, the tears freezing on my cheeks. My dish of watery soup and single slice of bread reassured me that the following day would definitely be the one.

It began, once again, with me carving a mark into the trunk and practising my aim. For the first time, I put my foot on the trunk in order to plan everything carefully and immediately noticed that it wasn't just an accurate strike that mattered, but also the angle of the axe. I focused on this new added difficulty and yet again postponed the execution of my plan. I cried with anger once again, unable to accept my own cowardice.

There was a guard waiting for me in my room and upon entering, he uttered just one word to me: '*karcer*'. This was a hole dug into the ground, with no window, just a small fireplace which was lit for an hour at a time to ensure the prisoner being held there didn't freeze to death. Due to my poor work performance, I was to spend the night there. My intention to injure myself was strengthened once more, and I swore that the next day, I was definitely going to do it.

When the day arrived, after two practice blows, I put my foot on the mark, took a swing, and struck with the axe. But somehow, my foot, guided by an invisible force, pulled out of the way. I'd got scared! The same thing happened multiple times, as my body subconsciously protected me from harm. In the end, my better conscience won out, something the war had taught me every time I received a nonsensical order. For the last time, I took a swing and struck. I'd done it! My foot hadn't recoiled and I felt relief at seeing an axe sticking out of my boot. I felt no pain, probably because my feet were stone-cold. Removing the axe, I could see that it had managed to hit the trunk between my two toes. It terrified me as I know I wouldn't be able to do it a second time. I had a different idea. I put my second toe under the axe blade and, with a huge hammer, hit the axe's handle. Blood gushed out everywhere, but I still felt no pain. I was saved!

I was transported back to the camp, but the injury wasn't bad enough to warrant a stay in hospital. Instead, I was given four weeks' sick-leave, during which time I was able to rest both physically and mentally. I didn't have to worry about the Karelian tundra, all I had to do was file a report to the Russian officer supervising the work and tell him about my accident. My explanation was a good one: I hadn't fully recovered from the tendonitis and my excuse meant I wouldn't be threatened by any investigation regarding self-harm. What's more, after having survived two accidents, I was able to apply for a job in a different commando. In the past, I'd always considered suicides to be cowards who refused to take responsibility for their own lives. Now I understood them much better.

Chapter 29

Fresh Meat

One day, eight new prisoners arrived having been transferred from the main camp in Petrozavodsk. They'd worked there as so-called 'pears' by carrying out transport-related jobs, but after a few misdemeanours had been sent here as punishment. After a few days, a rumour started circulating that they'd brought stolen goods with them and a huge search of the camp was ordered while we were all working at the brick factory. The whole camp was turned upside down and pieces of meat were found under the mattress of 18-year-old Heinz Schmidt. But the rumours were only partially true. First, the transport workers had had no contact with any meat, and second, Heinz Schmidt belonged to our crew, not to the 'pears' group. Despite this, as soon as he returned from work he was locked in the hole and told to confess where he'd found the meat. As it turned out, he'd killed the cat belonging to the Russian camp commandant, Captain Sutschkov. The cat had originally been taken from one of the railway transports in East Prussia and Sutschkov had given it to his wife as a gift. In the end, Schmidt received a fairly light punishment due to his poor condition. After all, the poor boy had only wanted some food. He was sentenced to five days in the hole, without food, but every mealtime he was dragged into the kitchen and forced to watch us devouring our soup. This 'light' punishment could have been fatal for him: the hole was a damp pit in the centre of the yard, covered only with a few planks. It was always dark and there wasn't enough room to stand up properly or even lay down. Fortunately, Schmidt was helped by the thriving sense of comradery in the camp and our interpreter, Alfred, from

Besarabia, threw him some food. Indeed, we all saved him something from our small rations. I should also mention Richard Salzgeber, who worked in the kitchen, as well as Juppie Scharfenkamp, who helped many others as well.

This whole unfortunate event led to wild outburst of rumours about the cat's demise, and Heinz Schmidt soon became famous throughout the camp.

Chapter 30

Deforestation

Winter arrived again, the tundra froze, and the swamps were accessible once more. The number of brigades working in the brick factory was reduced and the forest brigades were reformed. Every day, armed with saws and axes, and in temperatures of –20°C to –30°C, we were sent out into the forest, marching through metre-high snowdrifts and cutting down trees needed for construction, usually travelling about 6-7 kilometres every day. Completely exhausted, we would finally reach our destination, but then there was a whole eight hours of work ahead of us, not to mention the march back to the camp. Each of us had a target of 6 cubic metres of wood, but our physical condition made this impossible to achieve. Our strength would leave us hour after hour and in the afternoon we were barely able to lift our arms. Sometimes we would find some frozen mountain ash under the snow, which was perfect for replacing the lack of vitamins. But looking for it was strictly forbidden and we risked being hit with a rifle butt. The guards would yell at us in Russian: '*Charaszo raboti – skoro domoj!*'[52] We didn't know that our job was some form of penance and so they couldn't motivate us to work honestly. Indeed, it was quite the opposite, we would scheme and come up with various ideas just to meet the target.

The Karelian forest is very old and we would sometimes cut down trees that had over 320 rings in their trunks. Between the trees there were also trunks of dead ash trees, as well as alder trees

52. 'The faster you work, the sooner you'll be home.'

with thin branches, which our saws would cut through like paper. We came up with an idea of cutting each trunk into pieces, always stacking them at the end of the piles. That way, each pile had the required volume, but was also half-empty at the same time. Then when everything was loaded on to the trucks, the 'fake' cuts of wood would be thrown away and the whole process would start all over again. Unfortunately, it didn't last for long as the Russian supervisor soon noticed our scheme and informed the Russian officer in charge. As a punishment, our daily food ration was reduced to 200 grams of bread and the fourth-rate soup, the 'Ludwig', which was the best laxative around.

We were practically starving to death as our health deteriorated day by day. The other brigades weren't faring much better and soon half of the 380 people were unable to work. Eventually, a delegation from Moscow was sent to investigate the situation and immediately realised that the prevailing conditions weren't fit for living in – just as they were in many other camps. All of a sudden, the Russians

Painting by Richard Siegert showing prisoners working in the tundra.

decided they cared about their German workforce. Their whole system was under threat and we were the ones who were supposed to rebuild Russia. After this, conditions in the camp began to improve. Firstly, our working hours were reduced to eight hours per day and any additional work in the camp could only be for a maximum of two hours. Food rations were also to be controlled by German inspections. Our chances of survival, as well as our hopes, began to grow.

Chapter 31

Clay Making

Only the strongest prisoners were recruited for extracting clay as the entire brick factory that we'd constructed from scratch depended on them. At this point, the tundra was underwater and so after the summer, when work in the swamp was impossible, I was assigned to the first brigade, despite weighing only 53 kilograms. The brigade was famous for meeting 100 per cent of its targets, which meant they received 600 grams of bread and first-rate soup three times a day. The work was exhausting, but a very clever system had been devised to ensure that the required quotas were met every day. The target amount was 64 m^3 of clay for 18,000 bricks during eight hours of work. We used a rope hoist to pull out full bucket loads. At the beginning, we dug really deep into the ground, sometimes finding ourselves facing an almost 3-metre wall of clay. The work was as follows: half of the crew pressed a thin, horizontal line into the wall, then the rest hammered in metal poles along the marked-out area. Ropes were attached to the poles and with one swift movement we could pull away a thick layer of clay several metres thick, which was then loaded onto the waggons. Thanks to this method, none of us had to worry about breaking the clay individually.

In winter we worked underground and so weren't able to extract the clay in this way as the corridors were simply too low. We still wanted to meet the target, of course, but soon started to lose energy. We made a fire using an empty fuel barrel pushed into the wall, allowing us to work shirtless, even though the temperature outside reached -30°C. However, whenever the buckets needed emptying, someone had to go outside into the cold

One day, I fainted and blacked out. I was transported by wagon to the camp and from there to the infirmary. As it turned out, I wasn't just suffering from fatigue but also pneumonia, and so was taken to the hospital in Petrozavodsk where seven other patients with the same symptoms as me were in the same room. On the first day, each of us were given the antibiotic Sulfidin, a medicine universally loved by the Russians that originally came from American supplies. Unfortunately, this American antibiotic ran out and the next day we were only given quinine, which helped bring down our body temperature. Two of the patients had a bad reaction to the medicine and would regularly vomit afterwards, before dying soon after that. Considering we were all still prisoners, the hospital's food rations were fairly decent: we received 500 grams of bread and soup three times a day. I think about 600 grams of bread was the standard received in Russia at the time. During one of my follow up visits to the hospital, a Russian officer who spoke fluent German asked me if we were all being treated properly. When I asked him why in a Russian hospital the patients were given less bread than the norm, he replied: 'Those unable to work are unworthy of Russian bread'.

Chapter 32

'Potchemu'

This Russian word for 'why' was used as a nickname for our brick factory manager, so let me give you an example of why he was given such a name. The story takes place while we were storing the wood. We were unloading the trunks and putting them into piles, as usual, with our bare hands. The wheel hadn't yet been discovered, or was simply too expensive. One time, three of us were carrying a trunk, balancing it on our shoulders, when the manager noticed us. He bounded over in three or four steps, pulled the trousers of the man in the middle and screamed: '*Potchemu*? Why three men? Two men, two!' The other two men nearly collapsed under the weight of the trunk. According to him, no matter what the task, the smallest number of men should carry it out and his first question was always '*Potchemu*? Why so many men?' After two years (which was out of the reach of my imagination at the time) I beat '*Potchemu*' with his own weapon.

In the meantime, we not only cleaned the old bricks but also built a field kiln from them. We then fired new bricks in it which were used to build another, even bigger kiln. Thanks to their German workforce, a completely new brick factory was built that produced over a million bricks a month.

During one of our lunch breaks, one of my colleagues approached me and asked if I've seen '*Potchemu*', who was cutting wood. I was very surprised when he told me that our former supervisor had been sentenced to eight years' forced labour for embezzling Russian property and not only that, he had to serve his sentence at our brick factory. I went over to see him out of sheer curiosity, and there he was, together with an unfortunate companion, cutting metre-long logs. He let me watch for a little while before shouting: 'Why are you looking at me like that?!' Calmly and stoically I answered: '*Potchemu*? Why two men? One is enough!' He threw his axe at me, angrily. With my fingers crossed, symbolising jail, I added: 'Mr Supervisor, I'm a German prisoner of war and will soon be returning home, but you're a thief and have got eight years of this!'

I'll try to reconstruct the events leading to his conviction. The brick factory had to deliver 18,000 bricks per shift, which required 64 m^3 of clay. We worked three shifts, with the night shift working an hour less, adding up to 1.5 million bricks per day. The first count was made by a Russian woman and each cart heading into the drying room contained 400 bricks. The Russian woman noted everything down and made a mark on one of the bricks for the accounts. We knew she wouldn't be able to watch every vehicle closely for eight hours straight, and so decided to use this to our advantage. When she wasn't looking, we rotated the cart on the turning plate and then returned with the same cart again behind her back, meaning the same cart ended up being counted twice. All we had to do was replace the brick she'd marked and another 400 bricks had been 'counted'. Sometimes we were able to do this trick up to ten times during a shift, meaning the Russians then had 4,000 non-existent bricks in their account books. Thus, the clay mine extracted 64 m^3 of non-existent raw materials.

The second count was made by the people who unloaded the bricks from the kiln. We were supposed to stack 200 bricks on one pile for the Russian '*prorab*' to count, but each time he briefly left his post, we stacked the bricks that had already been counted back in the same place. Yet another trick that allowed us to meet our targets. This system, a testament to the Russian economy, had been developed to perfection, and after three years of our slave labour, a commission was sent to inspect the Russian bookkeeping. They calculated that a certain number of bricks were produced, as reported in the account books, but the number never matched the number of bricks delivered. It was clear to us that these were obviously the fictitious bricks that were never actually manufactured, but instead, the supervisor was accused of selling them on the black market. His excuses about the bricks being destroyed during the firing were of no use, because such a waste could easily be measured and calculated. Following the investigation, he was sentenced to eight years' forced labour for embezzling Russian property. I felt a wild satisfaction because he, too, had lied to us by manipulating the Russian targets, for which many of us had paid with our lives.

Chapter 33

Release from 'Paradise'

To my surprise, in 1948 I was transferred back to the main camp, where 2,000 men were still being held prisoner. Later, I would hear that our brick factory had been shut down and the crews put on a transport and sent back to the homeland. Russian prisoners, meanwhile, had taken over our work there.

In the main camp, one of the barracks was surrounded with barbed wire. It was the building where SS men were kept and was guarded by two armed soldiers. One day, they were transported on a ship to Lake Onega, where they would work in the tundra, chopping down the trees and repairing a damaged dam. The main camp was disbanded and the crew were sent home.

Before that, however, I was sent with some of the others to a different camp by the sea. Twice I had missed out on being on the list for people being sent home. I was almost certain that this was for political reasons as in previous years, I'd often been interrogated, sometimes in the middle of the night, and sometimes even taken away from my work for no reason. I remember it affecting me mentally at first, but eventually I just got used to it. My return home seemed to be miles away from me. Indeed, there were still 200 Austrians with me in the camp. Stalin had set them free back in 1947, but nevertheless, they still weren't on any of the return transports.

One day, we were told that our camp was being disbanded and everyone, apart from those whose names would be read out, would be released. Our hearts were beating like hammers. Suddenly, the man standing next to me collapsed upon hearing his name being

НКО–СССР От карантина освобожден.

Войсковая часть
Полевая почта
6194S
194 г.

СПРАВКА

Бывший военнопленный
Сигерт, Рихард, Рихард
(фамилия, имя, отчество)
года рождения освобожден из лагеря для военнопленных и следует по месту своего постоянного жительства в г.
д. Хинделанг р-н Сонтхофен

24 VIII 1949

место для печати

Командир в/ч Советской Армии
Полевая почта № 6194S

Г 2987 49

Antrag gemäß KgfEG. gestellt am 25. Juni 1954

Gemeindeverwaltung des Marktes Hindelang

Ungültig zum Bezug v. Lebensm. ...

Ministerium der Streitkräfte
UdSSR
Truppeneinheit
Feldpost-Nr.
194

AUSWEIS

Ehemaliger Kriegsgefangener
Siegert Richard
(Name, Vorname, Vatersname)
geboren am 1922 ist aus dem Kriegsgefangenenlager entlassen worden und befindet sich auf der Heimreise
nach Hindelang Kr. Sonthofen

Deutsche Reichsbahn
24. JUL 1949

21. JUL

(Stempel)

Kommandeur der Einheit der Sowjetarmee
Feldpost-Nr. 6194S

Documentation (in both Russian and German) showing Richard Siegert's release from the Russian camp allowing him to travel to Hindelang. (*Richard Siegert*)

called out. Death had set him free from any further physical and mental suffering. I sighed with relief when my name wasn't read out. It was the end of July 1949 and after this last, tragic episode, and nearly five years of captivity, I was finally a free man.

Gefreiter Alfred Leupold

Hetzer tank radio operator and loader during the battles for Poznań in January and February 1945.

I met Leupold after I was detained in Poznań, during my trip from the hospital in Mühlhausen, in Thuringia, to Olsztyn, where I was assigned to a reserve unit.

Like me, Leupold was also detained in Poznań. He'd been ordered to join his unit (I don't know which one exactly as I never asked him about it), which was a part of the '*Grossdeutschland*' division that wasn't deployed in Poznań. Instead, along with ten others, he was assigned to the 500th Training and Reserve Assault Gun Battalion. It was he who led me to *Oberfeldwebel* Sander and thanks to him I joined the Tiger's crew. Leupold, as a trained radio operator, joined the Hetzer crew.

We didn't meet again until around 8 February, when he appeared in front of the Citadel's North Gate. When asked about his actions in the battle for Poznań, he only told me that he'd been fighting in the Piątków neighbourhood. He also mentioned that four drivers from his crew had been shot by Russian snipers. I didn't ask him anything else, after all, everyone was busy with their own problems in that chaos.

On the night of 23 February, Leupold broke away with one of the groups through the Zeppelin Meadow, but was captured soon afterwards. We met again later on the meadow, at the assembly site where all prisoners of war from the area were brought. From then on we stayed together, even during 'propaganda march' through Poznań, and during our stay in the 'police camp'.

Gefreiter Alfred Leupold born 28 February1924, died 18 September 2001

From the 'police camp' we travelled on the same transport towards Karelia, and the main camp at Petrozavodsk, near Lake Onega. From there, the newcomers were sent to eighteen different camps, from Karelia to Murmansk. Leupold remained in the main camp while I was sent to the 'brick factory camp' in Sulasch-Gora. We'd finally been separated, but when the prisoners from the 'brick factory camp' were freed, I was sent back to the main camp where I met up with Fred again. After this, the prisoners in the main camp were released, while I, as a political prisoner, was sent to a camp in the city, and then another by the sea.

Fred Leupold came from the border town of Hof, in Oberfranken, and all of the trains going back home and heading west went through Hof. Before the war, Leupold had been educated at the railway school and after being released from captivity, had found a job as a stationmaster. When my train entered Hof station, Fred was standing there on the platform. Reunited once again, our friendship continued.

Richard Siegert

A friendship that lasted for over fifty years. Leupold and Siegert on a joint trip to the mountains. Hindelang, March 1975. (*Richard Siegert*)

Army Ranks of the SS, Waffen-SS, Wehrmacht and British/US Armies

SS and Waffen-SS	Wehrmacht	British/US Army
SS-Schütze	*Schütze*	Private
SS-Oberschütze	*Oberschütze*	Senior Private/Private 1st Class
SS-Sturmann	*Gefreiter*	Senior Private/Acting Corporal
SS-Rottenführer	*Obergefreiter*	Lance Corporal/Corporal
SS-Unterscharführer	*Unteroffizier*	Corporal/Sergeant
SS-Scharführer	*Unterfeldwebel*	Sergeant/Staff Sergeant
SS-Oberscharführer	*Feldwebel*	Staff Sergeant/Technical Sgt
SS-Hauptscharführer	*Oberfeldwebel*	Sergeant Major
SS-Sturmscharführer	*Stabsfeldwebel*	Regimental Sergeant Major
SS-Untersturmführer	*Leutnant*	2nd Lieutenant
SS-Obersturmführer	*Oberleutnant*	Lieutenant/First Lieutenant
SS-Hauptsturmführer	*Hauptmann*	Captain
SS-Sturmbannführer	*Major*	Major
SS-Obersturmbannführer	*Oberstleutnant*	Lieutenant Colonel
SS-Standartenführer	*Oberst*	Colonel
SS-Oberführer	no equivalent	no equivalent
SS-Brigadeführer	*Generalmajor*	Brigadier General/Brigadier
SS-Gruppenführer	*Generalleutnant*	Major General
SS-Obergruppenführer	*General der Infanterie*	Lieutenant General
SS-Oberstgruppenführer	*Generaloberst*	General
no equivalent	*Generalfeldmarschall*	Marshal
SS-Reichsführer	no equivalent	no equivalent

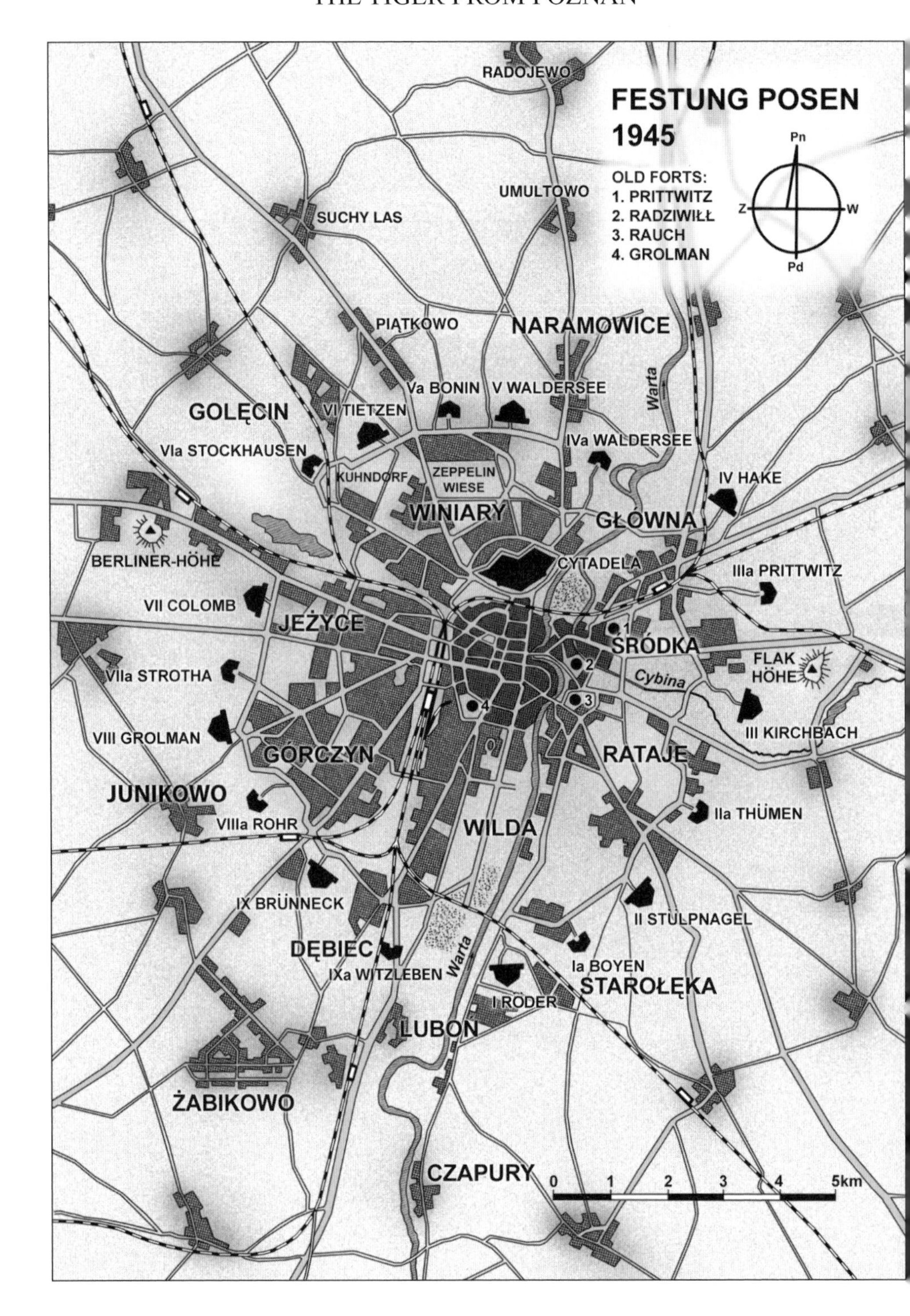
FESTUNG POSEN
1945
OLD FORTS:
1. PRITTWITZ
2. RADZIWIŁŁ
3. RAUCH
4. GROLMAN
Pn
Z
W
Pd
RADOJEWO
UMULTOWO
SUCHY LAS
PIĄTKOWO
NARAMOWICE
Warta
Va BONIN
V WALDERSEE
GOLĘCIN
VI TIETZEN
VIa STOCKHAUSEN
IVa WALDERSEE
KUHNDORF
ZEPPELIN
WIESE
IV HAKE
WINIARY
GŁÓWNA
BERLINER-HÖHE
CYTADELA
IIIa PRITTWITZ
VII COLOMB
JEŻYCE
ŚRÓDKA
FLAK
HÖHE
VIIa STROTHA
Cybina
VIII GROLMAN
III KIRCHBACH
GÓRCZYN
RATAJE
JUNIKOWO
IIa THÜMEN
VIIIa ROHR
WILDA
IX BRÜNNECK
II STÜLPNAGEL
DĘBIEC
Warta
Ia BOYEN
IXa WITZLEBEN
STAROŁĘKA
I RÖDER
LUBOŃ
ŻABIKOWO
CZAPURY
0
1
2
3
4
5km